MW00884583

Why Is the Soft Side the Hardest Part?

Reflections of an Executive Philosopher

William D. Mayo

AuthorHouse™
1663 Liberty Drive
Bloomington, IN 47403
www.authorhouse.com
Phone: 1-800-839-8640

First published by AuthorHouse 11/30/2011

ISBN: 978-1-4634-7440-9 (sc)
ISBN: 978-1-4634-7438-6 (e)
ISBN: 978-1-4634-7439-3 (dj)

Library of Congress Control Number: 2011915727

Printed in the United States of America

Most men die with their music still inside them.

Oliver Wendell Holmes

Contents

INTRODUCTION

I've often been called a philosopher, as if that's somehow a slur. I'll admit it always sounded like criticism each time it was voiced, but I really took no offense, and I never debated the label. In fact, I kind of liked it. I preferred to let my results defend my approach, and those results always steadfastly justified my philosophy.

This book is my story: the story of my philosophy as a leader, how it came to be, and how it's served those people and businesses I've led. It's a story that unfolded over the course of nine years in the US Navy, twenty-nine years in corporate America, and fifty-nine years on the planet. Following a brief military career as executive officer of a ship and battalion commander for over 900 recruits and senior noncommissioned officers, I resigned my commission to join one of America's industrial giants and most admired companies, Caterpillar, Inc.

At first blush, it seems unlikely that the military or the executive office of a Fortune 50 company would harbor a so-called philosopher in its ranks, and certainly not in its top echelon. The military is a bastion of discipline, duty, honor, and country, while businesses and boardrooms are typically the dominion of accountants, MBAs, finance types, and economists. Philosophers? Well, you don't typically find them cultivated in these endeavors.

I offer no apology for my philosophical bias. I realize it may have been considered out of place, even perhaps naïve at times within my executive sphere. Perhaps it was considered too soft, too gooey, and not sufficiently hard-nosed to produce results by some managers. I get that. I would often philosophize about loving people unconditionally, about selfless service, about courage and passionate authenticity, and about how these human attributes and emotions are the keys to unleashing deep, heartfelt commitment in employees. Yet while I may have created discomfort among some of my colleagues and provoked debate with those who would rather submit to the seduction of wooing Wall Street's favor, at the end of the day my philosophy did achieve results—outstanding results. And along the way it achieved the highest employee engagement in my company as well. I'll stand on that as affirmation of my approach.

In reality, when the right leadership philosophy embraces the so-called "soft side" to unleash the power of people, it liberates the most potent force imaginable. That kind of philosophy belongs in business. In fact, I believe that the philosophies I'll share with you buoyantly support the one thing all managers actually covet—results.

But just what is meant by the term *the soft side?* It is the people side of enterprise that is euphemistically (if not derisively) referred to as business's softer side. It is that aspect of business that deals with the human heart and how we interact with others to inspire them. Yet we often speak of developing soft skills such as communication, listening, diplomacy, creativity, and interpersonal skills as if these so-called softer topics are merely a side dish for the real meat of business. The implication is that greater importance resides in mastery of hard-core competencies, such as business acumen and economic, financial, or technical skills. But many managers I've known have confided that it's the soft side that is so challenging for them. And soft skills remain some of the most difficult to master. But master them we must, because the human side of enterprise is critical. People make businesses successful, and leaders must learn how to continually navigate soft-side challenges effectively to achieve extraordinary results.

Despite confidence in my approach and the notable results it achieved, I still often found myself wondering why some managers felt uncomfortable with a philosophy that acknowledged that people counted more than numbers. After all, what's so bad about being philosophical? What's the threat? Indeed, philosophy is nothing if not the reflective discussion of fundamental questions concerning the nature of reality, accepted knowledge, or espoused values. It has been called the *queen of sciences* because it always asks "why"? And the purpose of this book is to pose and answer just that question. Why? Why is the soft side, the people side of business, often the hardest part? Why are so many managers threatened by a philosophy that is rooted in the soft side rather than in the managerial or financial side of the ledger? And why is the soft side so often relegated to the bottom of the pile in deference to the bottom line?

These are questions worth pondering. In fact, the irony is that the key to achieving bottom-line results lies within the answers to these questions. This book strips away the managerial clutter and unearths the key leadership philosophies that leverage the power of people. And this power enables business to achieve better and more sustainable results while creating a legacy of new leaders in the ranks of those that follow.

Now despite my philosopher's label, let me set the record straight.

My training as a leader came not from pandering support groups or even liberal academia. I have not formally studied human organizational behavior or psychology in an academic setting. Nor have I taken a single philosophy course. My penchant for the so-called soft side and my philosophical musings about leadership were honed in the lab of human experience. They are not rooted in the theoretical or a research bias. Mine is a philosophy born in the trenches, where real business challenges beset the modern manager and leader in an ambiguous, change-laden world.

I studied an engineering discipline at the US Naval Academy. I served as executive officer and navigator aboard a US Navy combatant with a crew of over eighty crusty sailors and trained thousands of young navy recruits. And once in the business world, I rose through the ranks of one of corporate America's industrial giants and most admired companies, Caterpillar, Inc. I was elected an officer of the company in 2005. Hardly the résumé you'd think of as the normal path for a philosopher. But that was my journey, and along the way, I've learned a few things about leading people and achieving results.

I retired in 2008, although I prefer to call it my reallocation. Webster's defines retire as "to shrink away, retreat, or quit"; while reallocate means to "set aside for a special purpose." I have recently reallocated from corporate life and am currently teaching leadership at a small midwestern college. I serve on three corporate boards and provide consulting services to large and small businesses. What I've found lacking in the academic world, however, is also sadly lacking in the corporate world. Both might be producing competent managers, but they are woefully under-preparing future leaders. Ralph Nader said, "I start with the premise that the function of leadership is to produce more leaders, not more followers." So getting the soft side right springs to the top of the heap in importance rather than falling to the bottom of the pile.

Over the course of the next ten chapters, I will present my story and my leadership philosophies. I will compare my approach to the prevailing management practices I've observed in so many other executives. Certainly I've known successful managers who get results without being skilled in the soft side of business. In fact, some were downright hard-nosed. But I know they could have achieved more with less personal stress and less stress imposed on others if they'd only learned how to navigate the waters of the soft side. For those motivated by the bottom line, my story is a case for the soft side being the *most important contributor to business results,* and surprisingly it doesn't need to be the most difficult aspect of leading a business.

If you're still with me to this point, I'm encouraged. Your eyes are on this page, and that betrays your interest in answering the great whys of the soft side. It also suggests you inherently understand the importance of the people side of the equation and want to solve it. And that desire is the essential start to your journey.

To begin, here's an important philosophical conviction that underpins my entire philosophical approach: Managers manage things. Leaders lead people. If it's more management theory you are hungry for, you might want to select another book. If you want to *lead* people and *achieve* sustainable results, settle in. I promise a quick and uncomplicated read. In fact, I would argue that it's all relatively simple. Not easy perhaps, but simple to grasp. And it takes courage. Perhaps that's what actually makes the soft side so hard for some people. We overcomplicate it and are reluctant to courageously pursue it. Let's keep it simple and explore the realms of courageous application that make it work so profoundly.

The soft side is about people, and people are *not* things. Nor are people assets. Assets are objects that businesses consume, depreciate, and write off over time. Yet sadly, if you Google the phrase "People are our most important asset" you would find over twenty-one million entries, many of these from companies boasting that this credo reflects their commitment to people. It is a sorely misplaced philosophy. People are flesh and blood, emotional, human beings. And leaders need to understand that truth and lead accordingly. Employees want to be led, not managed.

So follow me and allow me to lead you to a different (and dare I suggest) better place. Without apology, I will offer you no proof in the form of statistical data, corroborating academic studies, or validated endorsements. I'll reference some leadership thought leaders, some well known and others whom you might find unlikely sources for leadership philosophy. But this is simply my story, written from my place of truth. And it is a place I invite you to examine. It's a place I invite you to be, a place from which you will lead people more effectively to yield better and more sustainable results for your business, for your shareholders, *and* for your team. And you *can* create a legacy that has your thumbprints all over it in the form of those leaders that come after you.

Oliver Wendell Holmes once said, "Most men die with their music still inside them." I believe a good leader is like a good musical conductor. A conductor doesn't play the instruments but merely helps the musicians perform better. When an effective human leader conducts people, culture, vision, and community and leads by example, the score can be a beautiful symphony. And after the notes are played, those that are keeping score will find the results very much worth counting.

As a final introductory note, let me explain my obvious use of song titles as chapter headings. Each chapter begins with an excerpt of lyrics from a song you're likely familiar with. In some way, all of these song lyrics relate to my philosophical approach, and I promise to make the correlation. But more than that, using song titles reflects my earnest hope that this book unbridles that symphony inside of you and liberates your inner leader. And as you undertake this journey through these pages by provoking your own personal reflection, it is my hope that you will also unleash the philosopher within you as well. Business could use a few more philosophers.

Chapter 1: We Gotta Get Out of This Place

Watch my daddy in bed a-dyin'
Watched his hair been turnin' grey
He's been workin' and slavin' his life away
Oh yes I know it
He's been workin' so hard,
yeah I've been workin' too, baby, yeah
Every night and day, yeah
We gotta get out of this place
If it's the last thing we ever do
We gotta get out of this place
Cause girl, there's a better life for me and you.
Words and music by Barry Mann & Cynthia Weil (1965)

The '60s were a time for questioning everything. Religion, war, politics, ethnic equality, patriotism, love, and even business were called into question. It was a time of burgeoning social revolution. Eric Burdon and the Animals recorded "We Gotta Get Out of This Place" in 1965, and it quickly became an anthem for the movement. Popular with armed forces personnel, it also became the theme song for Vietnam and those protesting the war.

Today corporate America is in its own battleground. A lack of confidence in business leaders, contempt for corporate greed, and the perception of ethics lost plagues enterprise today, even to the point of blaming the current economic crisis on these prevalent factors. The Animals' recording is yet today a fitting clarion call for a leadership philosophy focused on the soft side.

We need to win back the hearts of our people. Truly, business needs to get out of the place it is mired in today. But the management thinking that got us into this position won't lead us out. It will take a new approach—one that puts people above revenue targets, stock price, and the incessant counting of the corporate beans. And to that point, remember this little ditty from childhood?

Beans, beans ... the musical fruit.
The more you eat, the more you toot.
The more you toot, the better you feel.
So let's have beans for every meal!

As kids, we'd recite it and laugh at the invariable flatulence that followed a diet of those musical morsels. Many managers I've known are big advocates of beans, or at least bean *counting*. They apparently have the lyrics committed to memory as their mantra, fervently submitting to the religious dogma of more and more "bean counting." I'm not a numbers zealot. They have their place, but it seems to me that in many businesses today, managers are metric-crazed. Too many metrics merely create clutter *and* clatter, reminiscent of a runaway train. In my company, we never met a metric we didn't like. The more we had, the better we felt. So we had metrics for *everything*—a steady diet of metrics. Unfortunately, much like that musical fruit, they tended to be more gaseous than substantive.

During one overseas assignment, I worked for a talented manager who was insatiably hungry for the beans. He actually believed we needed to manage *116* top-tier metrics—*116!* And those were just the top tier of our runaway metrics train. The monthly staff meetings became a monotonous parade, if not charade, of metrics. So much so that many times, that's all we had time to cover. Numbers. We didn't talk about employees. We didn't talk about customers. We talked about numbers. I found my eyes glazing over as chart after chart of "Red/Yellow/Green" scorecards and the attendant rationalizations droned on. In my mind, those scorecards were an incessant assault against what was important—things like culture, people, and customers.

I would often argue, though unsuccessfully, that the Creator gave me only ten fingers. Perhaps that would be a good maximum number of key metrics to track. However, this manager's need to control—or unfortunately his illusion of control—kept the focus on numbers and incessant metrics. He would always quip, "What gets measured gets done." But guess what? All those metrics did not improve results. As divisions go, his was the poorest performing marketing unit within the firm. I guess what got done was *not* what got measured, was it? As a European colleague and I would muse, "Ouzan ou gaz"—which literally means—"emitting a gaseous air." It may have been funny, but it's actually more than a little sad; a sad commentary on management's obsession with numbers at the expense of people.

This manager's mantra was trumped by the simple reality that all the scorekeeping in the world wouldn't improve the health of his division. All it did was drive tedious administrivia and score keeping—and it kept our accountants gainfully, if not productively, employed. Furthermore, every staff meeting could devolve into a tense gathering where managers found themselves gloating or sweating. They would sit there, unengaged at best, or gloating at worst—when their metrics were green—while the "red" guys were sweating in the hot seat, hoping for cover from some other poor sot whose red was even redder than his. Talk about a gaseous waste of resources and valuable time together! We could have been talking about the business, but instead we made love to the numbers.

Many managers fall victim to his type of thinking. Rampant metrics mania only creates a cloud of confusion, not clarity. And it also creates a certain "gotcha" culture that causes employees to seek cover from red scores, or worse yet, to become complacent and take solace from those that are green. Think about it this way: The whole red/yellow/green thing implies traffic control. The law. But it's control gone amuck, and it isn't leadership. Although I certainly realize that not all metrics are bad, the trick is to track only the *right* metrics and not become seduced by all possible measures.

Philosophically, how do metrics relate to the soft side? And what leadership approach should be used to keep score? Here's the deal: philosophically, numbers matter, but people matter more. You can create all kinds of ways to count the score. But leaders avoid the seduction of chasing numbers that seems to entrap many an otherwise good manager. Good leaders learn how to integrate the numbers with the soft side. After all, leaders do know how to count, but they should know that people count more. My philosophy? If we take care of people—employees, colleagues, and customers—the numbers will take care of themselves. People make the business run, and they (like you) want to know what's going on too. So finding the right metrics serves not only the leader but also the employees, and I would argue that it helps customers as well. We do need to evaluate whether or not we're hitting the mark, are making progress, or are exceeding the business plan. That information is just as important to your employees as it is to you, your superiors, and your shareholders. The key is creating a culture where everyone not only knows the score but also knows how their personal contributions impact the score.

Philosophy @ Work

As vice president of Caterpillar's largest marketing unit, I enlisted the help of employees to identify what metrics mattered and what metrics were merely producing a bloated, gaseous scorecard. When I took over the position, we had over one hundred metrics! I wanted only a maximum of ten. With their input, we ended up with a one-pager of twenty. Still, a far cry better than one hundred-plus! Not too onerous for a ten billion dollar-plus division, either. This philosophical approach when applied within my team conveyed to the employees that we were focused on simplification, on chasing what really mattered. We were not merely in a beauty contest to "look pretty"; we were running a business focused on market leadership, profitable growth, and customer loyalty. When they believed that this focus was genuine and that they would be safe to focus on the key metrics that mattered, they committed much more passionately to the process of executing our mission. As for scorekeeping, it mattered, but they finally didn't feel smothered any longer by tedious tracking of numbers. This approach simplified the business and improved our focus on efforts that translated to the true purpose of our service. We grew market share, revenue, and customer loyalty by all measures. Employees were energized by the effort, goals were clarified, and buy-in was significantly enhanced because they were a part of shaping the focus for the division.

I stumbled into my metrics philosophy by accident. Years ago, I read an article in *INC Magazine*. It was the April 1989 issue, to be precise. It was entitled "Dream Team" and was similar in concept to a baseball draft for a fantasy league. *INC* unapologetically published their "Dream Team" of managers to run a fantasy new start-up. I was impressed with their selection for chief operating officer—a young man (forty years old at the time) by the name of Jack Stack. Jack was cofounder and CEO of Springfield Remanufacturing Center Corp., a forty million dollar former division of International Harvester.

INC labeled Stack a "revolutionary." Being a closet rebel myself and already beginning to realize that I was a bit of a square philosophical peg in a round corporate hole, I was intrigued. Stack was credited with an uncanny ability to engage a work force. He termed it "management by the numbers." When I read that, however, my initial reaction was to roll my eyes, fearing that here again was a numbers freak. But his unique way of engaging employees from shop sweepers to managers fascinated me. I read on. His approach was simply to convert employees at every level into businesspeople. *INC Magazine* stated, "His philosophy was certainly not anti-metrics. In fact, his philosophy was to publish the critical few metrics to the business for every employee to see."

Jack understood that people not only wanted to know the score but also wanted to know how their individual performance *contributed* to the key metrics for success. With his practical and transparent approach, people across the firm understood the business, knew which metrics were important to define success, and more importantly, knew how they individually contributed to that success. I also took note that Stack's culture allowed metrics to be set by the team. The desired targets were not established behind closed doors. Transparency in setting the targets and transparency in sharing the rewards comprised his approach. That philosophical approach resonated with me, and I made a pledge right then to lead with that philosophy going forward.

The second key point regarding metrics comes not from some

leading-edge managerial theory but from the edgy humor of cartoonist Gary Larson. It's not scholarly perhaps, but it is brilliant. And it illustrates my philosophy of establishing vision, metrics, and rewards. The cartoon depicts two spiders sitting atop a child's sliding board railing. They've spun a web across the bottom of the slide, intended to catch their prey as it swooshes down the sliding board gleefully unaware of the spider's trap below. The caption depicts one spider's comment to the other: "If we pull this off, we'll eat like kings!" These cartoon spiders provide a poignant lesson for business leaders. Be bold, have clear, *outcome-based* metrics, and help people understand the reward for achieving those goals.

As famed Chicago architect Daniel Burnham said, "Make no small plans; they have no magic to stir men's blood." Metrics should not only be the right measures, but they should also be bold, with a clear line of sight as to how everyone wins and shares in the rewards of achievement. The focus should be on the culture and the people so that they see what's in it for them. Again, if you take care of people, the numbers will take care of themselves. And when people understand the endgame, they'll self motivate to achieve it.

Unfortunately, businesses too often get sidetracked by measuring the trivial many. In the cartoon, as an example, a typical metric set might include 1) the time to construct the web, 2) the productivity of the spiders spinning the silk, 3) the thickness of the silk that ensures maximum retentive hold on the captive, 4) the rate of ascent and descent of the target, 5) the angle of the sun to ensure the web does not glisten. And so on and so on and so on. My philosophy is to keep it simple and focus on the *outcome* we want to achieve, not all the myriad methodologies to get there. I'll never forget a poster-child example of getting sidetracked by metrics mania.

Here's the context: Caterpillar dealers are legendary for providing outstanding customer support. With over 50,000 employees in the North American network of nearly sixty dealers, well over 75 percent of those employees are in the product-support side of the business. Caterpillar's dealer network is the envy of competitors. These dealers employ twice the capital in the business as the top four competitive distributor networks *combined.* We had a saying within the firm that the sales department sells the first machine but the product support department sells the rest. Clearly, Cat dealers set a world-class benchmark for providing outstanding customer service.

Yet my company once launched a dealer service excellence program aptly named "Images of Excellence." It was just that—an *image.* None of the methodology metrics contained in the program actually had any statistical correlation to what the customer wanted, such as service problems fixed on time, correctly the first time, and for a reasonable cost. That's what our customers told us they valued. But rather than simply measure a score of dealer excellence tied to those criteria, we also had a plethora of "how to" metrics—getting so detailed as to specify *how* we wanted the dealer to achieve the outcome. It was part of a comprehensive (if not invasive) factory program to measure everything from lines being painted on the service bay floors to outlined tool storage pegboards to the size of the customer waiting room, the mechanics' break room, and even whether or not coffee and refreshments were available. Don't get me wrong. These things might be nice to have, but *excellence*, as defined by the customer, had nothing to do with these prescribed methods. It was solely about fixing the service problem the first time, on time, and for a reasonable cost. From our desks in corporate, we apparently saw excellence differently and as a result got swept away in a tidal wave of metric foam. As author John le Carré wrote, "From behind the desk is a dangerous place from which to view the world." We even went so far as to specify the level of foot-candles of light in the repair bay. I'll never forget it. Seventy-five foot candles of light! As if mistakes aren't made in good lighting? Get real!

It's reminiscent of the Hawthorne Works productivity studies of the mid-1920s in Cicero, Illinois. At this manufacturing plant, lighting intensity was altered to examine its effect on worker productivity. The findings were not significant. It seemed as if the workers actually tried harder when the lights went dim, just because they knew that they were in an experiment and being observed. This phenomenon came to be known as the Hawthorne Effect. Simply stated, it said short-term productivity could be improved with "concerned management observation." In other words, people will behave differently when they are being watched. Duh!

But rather than prescribing how to perform every little aspect of a service repair, imagine if we had defined excellence in the same terms as the customer defined excellence and published those measures for everyone on the shop floor to see! I am convinced that it would have achieved the desired outcome far better and more sustainably than our short-lived *Images* program. That program died, thankfully, in short order, suffocated by the weight of too many prescriptive methodologies and assigned metrics. Paradoxically, the actual image in the eyes of those dealers attempting to deploy it was that it was just one more lame idea from corporate that passed like so much gaseous vapor.

My Soft-Side Philosophical Nugget:

Why is the soft side the hardest part when it comes to metrics? We make it harder than it has to be when we take our eye off the ball of what is really important. Leaders never chase numbers at the expense of people. We as leaders have to get out of the place where metrics and numbers count more than people. The leader's focus should be on liberating people to achieve extraordinary results, not limiting them by excessive management control. If you take care of people, the numbers will take care of themselves. Leaders must involve people in the target setting, focusing on outcomes and the few key metrics that are relevant. Don't chase methodologies; but rather specify desired outcomes. And certainly don't constrain the innovation and creativity of your people in pursuing the desired outcomes of your vision. Be bold. Stir people's imagination and paint a picture that illustrates how their individual performance contributes to success and to serving the customer better. Be transparent, and share the rewards. And remember—get out of the place that creates excessive metrics as an illusion of control. There is a better place out there for you and your people where their contributions and their emotional discretionary commitment are clearly tied to the significant few metrics that matter for success for the business.

Chapter 2: Cruel To Be Kind

Though you say you're my friend
I'm at my wits end
You say your love is bonafide
But that don't coincide
With the things that you're doing
When I ask you to be nice
You say you gotta be
Cruel to be kind, in the right measure
Cruel to be kind, it's a very good sign
Cruel to be kind, means that I love you
Baby, you gotta be cruel to be kind
Words & Music by Ian Gomm & Nick Lowe (1989)

Let's talk about some truths for a moment that must not be sidestepped. One truth is that some managers, when they hear the term *soft side,* are immediately skeptical. Perhaps they fear that it signals a time for group hugs or handholding teams singing "Kumbaya." It sounds foreign in the workplace. It feels uncomfortable, even wimpy. Indeed, it may seem as if a philosophy focused on the soft side belongs anywhere but in a hardcore business environment. As good friend and leadership coach Stan Slap once said, "Businesses are nothing more than self-serving economic entities." This hardly sounds like an environment conducive to leading with heart and focused on the people side of business. But here's another truth: The soft side is anything but soft. There is actually nothing soft about it; it is inordinately hard. My philosophy is centered on the people that make business work. It is a philosophy that enables creation of meaningful emotional commitment among employees and teams to achieve outstanding results. But without question, my philosophy did not permit me to ignore the leadership requirement to do some very difficult things. In fact, paradoxically, it emphatically implored me to tackle those uncomfortable issues that invariably arise when leading people.

Business, indeed life, is not a consequence-free zone. As an old axiom says, the truth hurts. But I note with comfort that ancient scripture also claims the "truth will set you free" (John 8:32 NIV). This is nowhere more evident than when leading people with integrity and authenticity. As a leader, confronting people with truth can be extremely difficult for the leader as well as the employee, especially when truth must confront an employee's poor performance, failure, or ethics. There is no place for cruelty in the work place, but it is even crueler to varnish truth or to spin it disingenuously when confronting issues with employees. Ignoring the truth patronizes the workforce, weakens the business, and undermines the leader. If speaking harsh truths is cruel, I submit that it ultimately is more kind than avoiding that truth. That is not a soft-side leader's philosophy; that's merely soft and cowardly. A genuine soft-side leader confronts the truth and speaks it without apology, especially when dealing with employees.

People will make mistakes. People will disappoint. People will behave unethically at times and sometimes will be irresponsible. And sometimes, people will fail. When these behaviors manifest in the work environment, there are consequences for the individual, consequences for the team, consequences for the business, and consequences for the leader. Indeed, there *must* be consequences, and these cannot be glossed over simply because a leader is committed to the *soft side* and leading with heart. In my view, a soft-side philosophy must be even more committed to truth and integrity in dealings with all employees as the leader unwaveringly faces and speaks truth as a vehicle to better serve employees, customers, teammates, colleagues, and ultimately, the business. This might be speaking the truth about a flawed program or initiative. It might be the truth about an employee's advancement potential. It might be the truth about the quality of or pricing for a product. Yet many times, revenue pressures, cost pressures, and political pressures make speaking truth a risky endeavor; nonetheless, authenticity requires it. A commitment to people requires it, and it is not easy, but there can be no escape. A leader committed to the soft side is likewise committed to speaking the truth in every circumstance. There is nothing soft about it, but it's more kind than shrinking from the consequences by spin or "making nice" to get along. It takes courage.

Although I often philosophize about there being an important place for love in the workplace, I'm speaking about a form of tough love that never shrinks from insisting upon the highest standards of personal and employee accountability. I think the primary reason managers shrink from this word, omit it from our leadership lexicon, or worse, exclude the emotion altogether from human engagement in the workplace is because we have a wrong-headed notion about what love means in the context of leading others or leading business.

It is certainly not love based on feelings of attraction, as love based on feelings is focused on self-benefit rather than benefit for another. Nor is it love based merely on friendship between people. While friendship may be the foundation for many successful relationships, being a leader does not mean that you must befriend everyone. It is not about merely being friends. When I speak of a leader loving his people, I am speaking of a selfless love, based on service to others without self-benefit. I am speaking of being truthful. To truly unleash the potential of others, to serve them and to help them grow, a leader must love in this unconditional way. Much like parenting, however, leaders set boundaries, set expectations, provide encouragement, implement discipline, provide guidance, and have performance standards with both accountability and consequences.

A philosophy rooted in the soft side does not mean being a leader who is soft on accountability. Quite to the contrary: a leader focused on the soft side doesn't merely offer a loving pat on the back or a sympathetic ear or look the other way. A leader confronts each situation directly, strongly, and decisively with unwavering commitment to the principle of accountability *and* the consequence for one's actions.

Philosophy @ Work

As a new vice president in 2005, I was confronted with a problem brought to me by a department manager and the human resources manager. A twenty-year employee, a senior middle manager, was discovered in an ethics violation. He was falsifying mileage reimbursement claims and pocketing around seventy-five dollars per month. When discovered, prior records were audited and the investigation revealed that this had been going on for three months. Both the department manager and HR manager advised me that this incident was "behind" the employee, that he was deeply repentant, and that he vowed to never do it again. They also suggested that he was experiencing personal issues at home that no doubt led to his lapse of ethical behavior.

The decision to deal with the employee's behavior was a local business unit discretionary matter, meaning that I was the decision maker. I had various disciplinary options, up to and including discharge. Of course, I asked them both for their input, and they recommended leniency, a temporary suspension. I told them that I would consider their input and get back to them by the end of the day. Later that day, this employee's wife, whom I knew personally, called me and sobbed about her husband's earnest repentance and begged me for leniency.

After considering the matter at length, at day's end I called the department manager and HR manager into my office to share my decision. I informed them that I was deeply saddened by the incident, and yet as a senior manager, this employee certainly knew the rules and our standards for ethical behavior. A further concern was that during the course of the investigation, a number of division employees were interviewed and knew of the incident. While my decision would be painful for the employee, I told them I must consider the impact on the 485 other employees of the business unit. As a result, I felt it best to terminate the individual's employment. My rationale was simple.

If 485 employees knew (and they always know) that I winked at such an ethical lapse—even though only seventy-five dollars per month—then I would be signaling to them that all future matters involving personal integrity of an employee were bordered by very blurry and subjective lines. The ethical standard of no stealing must mean no stealing. Zero tolerance. I terminated his employment. Of course, I provided outplacement support and family counseling and offered this to the employee in person. It was not an easy moment for me.

Clearly, this was not a soft approach but a rather hard-line approach to the consequences for unethical behavior.

> *Although committed to the people side of business, I felt I must choose the more difficult option. This was the only clear way I could stand for integrity and honesty as a standard for our business unit. Without question, it strained my heart to realize this employee's anxiety about losing his job after twenty years of service. But the soft side does not mean soft. And I did, in my mind, the more difficult but right thing.*

In every circumstance where people or businesses make choices or take action, there are consequences. I've always said that people have nearly infinite choices in any moment of decision, yet there is a finite set of attendant consequences tied to each choice. These are inescapable, and a soft-side leader *never* permits an employee to escape accountability for their actions nor evades accountability for himself or the business when either do not live up to ethical standards or principles. I'm not speaking of overt punishment, but it is not cruel to hold people accountable. I am speaking of a leader's courage to confront an individual with truth—be that person a subordinate or a superior—the truth that will allow them to learn, albeit sometimes painfully, but also the will set them free from the lingering pain of chronic mistakes or chronic disappointment, under performance, or false expectations and misaligned self-perceptions.

My Soft-Side Philosophical Nugget:

Why is the soft side the hardest part when it comes to leading with heart? We make it harder than it has to be when we evade the truth and consequences of people's actions, including our own. We make it harder than it has to be when we ignore the power of emotion to connect with people and inspire their passionate commitment. However, emotional connection does not imply license to avoid tough consequences when warranted.

When a leader provides an environment of emotional safety and yes, I dare say love, to the work team, he encourages risk taking, builds trust, and liberates emotional commitment among employees. Employees who are emotionally connected to the team provide unbridled discretionary effort. Every employee wants to know how to thrive, be safe, and prosper. I believe that this type of environment can only be created when leaders dare to bring their own personal emotional power and impact to the workplace. And this springs not from the head, not from the intellect, but from the human spirit— the heart. We call it love. Mother Theresa said, "It is not how much we do, but how much love we put in the doing. It is not how much we give, but how much love we put in the giving." She further stated, "Love cannot remain by itself. It has no meaning. Love has to be put into action, and that action is service." Such love is not gooey, soft, or namby-pamby love. It is love offered unconditionally and liberally but with an unwavering commitment to accountability and consequences for all. To do less is not love or service; yet sadly, it is all too common.

Chapter 3: Elusive Butterfly

You might have heard my footsteps
Echo softly in the distance through the canyons of your mind
I might have even called your name as I ran searching after something to believe in
You might have seen me runnin'
Through the long abandoned ruins of the dreams you left behind
If you remember something there
That glided past you followed close by heavy breathing
Don't be concerned; it will not harm you
It's only me pursuing something I'm not sure of
Across my dreams with nets of wonder I chase the bright elusive butterfly of love

Words & Music by Bob Lind (1966)

My brother David has always described himself as living in a perpetual state of suspended adolescence. He once said, "If you can remember the '60s, you didn't live them." Well, I was a mere fourteen years old in 1966, but I remember when Bob Lind's song "Elusive Butterfly" hit the airwaves. I thought it was wonderful. Certainly not the rock 'n' roll fare I normally tapped my toes to, but there was something magical in the lyrics—something beckoning. Years later, I learned what it was, and it became my anthem for an important philosophical credo about the importance of transformative change. That philosophy? *Chase the butterfly.*

So why chase the butterfly? As background, let me relate to you what Jack Kemp said in a 2008 speech to the Beavers (a heavy-engineering construction association). He said that American capitalism has lost its way. He pointed out that the basis for capitalism was never greed. It was (and still should be) *service*. Service is what business is all about, and importantly, Abraham Lincoln reminds us that leadership is all about service as well. He once said, "To lead you must first serve." But we've lost that mantra these days. We've taken our eye off of service to the customer in favor of an eye toward Wall Street. Perhaps some managers have never fully accepted that service to employees is the right leadership philosophy from which all excellence springs. But it is the right approach and will reap outstanding results.

Philosophy @ Work

I always appreciated how Mr. J. Irwin Miller, the son of one of Cummins Engine Company's founders, put it. He said it this way: "We are not in business to make money. We are in business to serve the customer. To the degree we do that better than competition, the customer rewards us with his dollars. To the degree we run an efficient operation, we reward ourselves with profit." This gives business the proper leadership perspective. It's not about the self-serving economic entity called "the business." It's about service to others.

Miller's is a beautiful, service-oriented philosophy. It's analogous to living and breathing. You don't wake up to breathe. But you need to breathe to wake up. So I clearly understand that businesses must make money to thrive and prosper. But they do so by providing value and service to their clients, not by chasing profits. Too often, businesses focus on the pursuit of money. Money is the result of pursuing the provision of value and service, just as breathing is the result, not the aim, of being alive.

Yet many times, when I would quote Miller's philosophy, I saw other managers' eyes become glassy with incredulity at my apparent naiveté. Apparently, I lost them at "We're not in business to make money." Sadly, the conscience of business seems to have been increasingly silenced by the relentless pursuit of wealth. In other words, as Kemp said, "Capitalism has lost its way." Business has spun a seemingly silky cocoon with threads of greed. While inside, the chrysalis actually needs transformative change. But it cannot happen without leadership. And the lesson of leadership we need comes from the butterfly.

Some years ago, I learned from a friend and coach of mine, Dianna Anderson, about the amazing science of transformation from caterpillar to butterfly. Specifically, I learned about something she termed "imaginal cells." Norie Huddle writes beautifully of this transformative process in her book, *Butterfly.* She explains how imaginal cells in a cocooning caterpillar hold the vision of the future butterfly. Despite the fact that these cells are first perceived as foreign invaders and are destroyed by the creature's own immune system, the imaginal cells continue to multiply and connect with a strength and force that ultimately and miraculously transforms the caterpillar into a beautiful future state. Some businesses—those that are content with their apparent security as caterpillars—are in desperate need of transformative change. And they need leaders who have the DNA and the courage to be imaginal cells. Courage is the operative word, because it is sadly true that you may be attacked—attacked by those resistant to change and by those who are comfortable in the cocoon of greed and the chrysalis of Wall Street. That's why today this line from Bob Lind's lyrics still resonates with me. *I might have even called your name as I ran searching after something to believe in.*

Remember when you left college and joined your first company? Remember the wide-eyed (and perhaps naïve) wonder you felt as you entered the workforce determined to make a difference? What happened? So many times, noble aspirations are squelched by the bureaucracy of management and by the self-serving economic realities of businesses that have forgotten they exist to serve. I firmly believe that people want to belong to something bigger than themselves.

Philosophy @ Work

I remember that during one particular speech I gave in 2007, I made this same point. I said that all people want to belong to something nobler, more worthwhile than just chasing money. I asked the audience how many were inspired by our company's vision to be a "100 billion dollar company by the year 2020." Predictably, many hands went up. As those first few hands rose, others in the audience looked around, and soon enough, virtually all hands in an auditorium of 250 people were raised high. Although I expected this politically correct response, I was disappointed. After a lengthy pregnant pause, I said, "That doesn't inspire me at all." You could have heard a pin drop. Then I asked them, "What company grew from about thirteen billion dollars in sales to over one hundred billion dollars in sales from 1996 to 2001?" The answer? Enron. I asked them how many were inspired by their example. No hands were raised.

Thankfully, my firm also had another vision statement—a noble statement of purpose that gave meaning to my service. It was "to be an admired global leader making progress possible around the world." That, I told the group, was inspirational. That was worth getting up for in the morning. That was worth my discretionary effort—my service; worth my heart; worth every ounce of creativity and passion I could muster. Caterpillar, Inc., is one of America's most admired companies. It has a world-renowned brand, wonderful dealer partners, and a global market share that is the envy of competitors. I was inspired to work for this global leading firm. Its products and the outstanding relational selling and customer service of its dealer organization were something to be immensely proud of.

I am adamant that all people want to—indeed need to—belong to something bigger and nobler than themselves. And it isn't the pursuit of wealth or the creation for the shareholder. Those are important elements of a well-run company, to be sure. But that should not be the sole aim and indeed is *not* the aim most employees will be inspired by. They will not derive purpose from the bulging girth of the cocoon or from spinning more golden threads. They will be inspired when they know in their hearts that their individual contributions have meaning and purpose. Ray Kroc said, "One of life's richest blessings is the opportunity to work hard at work worth doing." I believed, as do all Caterpillar employees, that the work we do, the products and services we provide, make the world a better place. And that is measured not in financial terms but by the quality of life Cat products enable around the globe.

American capitalism today needs to be transformed. It has lost its way. But to achieve that transformation, people need to be inspired. To transform the company into a truly service-oriented, customer-centric company, we need imaginal cells. We need people who are so committed to the vision and mantra of customer service that they essentially infect those other cells in the cocoon. Eventually, when enough imaginal cells are present, the transformation will occur. But it can *never* occur if the imaginal cells don't band together, or if in fear, they shrink from their noble purpose. And it will never occur if an imaginal leader doesn't inspire and define the vision of what can be. True, there is risk that "manager cells" will kill off any mutants one by one. And each leader must be aware that changing culture—more specifically, liberating people to transform culture—is an elusive objective. In my own experience, people earn their cynicism honestly. Besieged by program after program, they grow weary. A new leader coming into a position and talking about cultural change risks being labeled as just the new dog coming in to mark his corner. Cultural change envisioned by the leader may be resisted, met reluctantly, or accepted by employees as just one more flavor-of-the-month initiative.

In spite of all that, chase the butterfly. Be an imaginal cell. It will not harm you. It will liberate innovation in others, and you will find other imaginal cells eventually. And you will clump together, forming clusters that will be difficult to ignore. Soon there will be too many for the managerial cells to kill off. And you will be leading a transformative change within the chrysalis, displacing the managerial cells of self-serving greed with a more noble, humble, service-oriented, and customer-centric culture. In time, an entirely new entity will emerge. But again, I recognize that it is not without its risks. I'll never forget facing down another accusation hurled at me by a fellow executive who said, "You love your customers more than you love your shareholders." And to that I said "Amen."

My Soft-Side Philosophical Nugget:

Why is the soft side the hardest part of transforming culture? We make it harder than it has to be when we forget that capitalism is rooted in service and that each business actually has a more noble purpose than merely making money. That noble purpose begins with providing valuable products and services that customers need. People will achieve extraordinary results when their passions are aligned to that purpose. Businesses do not exist to make money alone. They exist first and foremost upon the principle of providing value—providing a valuable product or service. When business leaders put that first, good results will always follow.

Today's true leaders must often swim upstream against the tide of corporate greed and against the current of those who would pander to Wall Street expectations at the expense of the longer term. You must be brave, perhaps even philosophical, to chase the butterfly, transforming culture along the way. Become an imaginal cell and infect your colleagues and employees with a beautiful vision of your possible future state. Enlist other imaginal cells. Clump and cluster together. Remember that revenues and profits are only a result, not the aim of business. And remember that people want to commit to something that provides them with purpose, an opportunity to contribute to something bigger than themselves to make the world a better place.

So yes, chase that butterfly. Hold high your "nets of wonder" and endeavor to create a culture within your company where this philosophy is encouraged in all employees. Serving them in this way unleashes their creativity, passion, and innovation to be supremely focused on serving the customer better than their competition. Soon you will hear the footsteps of customers running through the meadows to find you. For customers, like your employees, want something to believe in. They too, want to catch the butterfly.

Chapter 4: Can't Buy Me Love

I'll give you all I got to give if you say you love me too
I may not have a lot to give but what I got I'll give to you
I don't care too much for money,
Money can't buy me love
Words and Music by John Lennon / Paul McCartney (1964)

They say that what goes around comes around. And lately, what seems to be coming around is the topic of employee engagement. It seems to be *the* hot topic these days, although I hadn't realized committed employees had *ever* gone out of style. So perhaps it's merely the term "engagement" that is hot and new. Frankly, I've always found the phrase employee engagement annoying. Perhaps I don't like the label because it's uttered in the language of management, not leadership. I prefer to think of employee engagement as four-letter word. More accurately, it's a four-letter acronym for me: LEAD. But I'll share more about this later.

One thing is certain ... with the new management focus on engagement comes the inescapable penchant to keep score and to manage it. While that aspect is anathema to me, if that's the only reason employee engagement has climbed the charts of management's hit parade, so be it. It is important because engaged people make business work. In my mind, all the better that even the metrics hounds are looking for solutions to improve it.

But I prefer to believe that businesses get it, and at some level desire to leverage the power of people while creating cultures where people thrive, are safe, and can prosper. That is clearly an admirable aim. Yet I admit that I have become more than a little skeptical about motives merely to improve engagement scores. That sounds like managers chasing metrics to me. And that just won't cut it.

Inspirational leadership creates employee engagement. I have an acronym that philosophically I consider the key to the not-so-cryptic solution to drive up those coveted scores. More importantly, it will also fundamentally improve the work environment for people. And a good employee environment is undeniably good for business.

The acronym? It's simple. LEAD: Love. Empowerment. Authenticity. Development. When leaders love their people, when they empower them, when they are authentic, and when they put time, energy, and effort into developing their employees to become leaders in their own right—well, engagement scores take care of themselves. Let's examine each of the letters of the acronym.

L: One of my leadership credos is to "strive to treat people like dogs." I know it sounds alarming initially. I've told many an employee and many management teams this credo, and the initial reaction is always the same: raised eyebrows, arched in suspicion, alarm, or disbelief. It certainly doesn't *sound* like a good people strategy until you go beyond the initial shock to reflect upon what it truly means. My premise is simple: we typically treat dogs *better* than we treat people!

So let me ask you. Do you (or did you ever) have a dog? If so, how did you treat it? How did it treat you in return? Here's the nearly universal scenario I've encountered when sharing this seemingly incongruent concept.

First, you play with your dog. They know you when you're laughing, being playful, engaging yourself in their world. They see you at your best. But still, you do not fail to give your dog clear expectations, such as, "Don't sit on the furniture. Don't do your mess on the carpet. Don't jump on the bed." Very clear expectations. Employees frequently lament that they all too often are left wondering just what the boss's expectations are for them. Ambiguity reigns, and clarity is elusive.

Next, let's say you return from work after a long, tough day and there's trusty Fido. He has delighted you with his performance. He's been mindful and careful with every clear instruction. What would you say? "Good dog! Great dog! I knew you could do it. You're such a smart doggie!" But conversely, let's say your dog does some of those undesirable things—that it violates your rules or falls short of your clear expectations. Then what do you say? "Bad dog! I told you not to do that!" In other words, you provide immediate feedback, either praise, or shall we say constructive feedback for improvement? You certainly *don't* save up all your disappointments for the dog's annual performance appraisal. You don't speak behind its back to other doggies and ruin his doggie career. You don't sabotage him in the doggie succession-planning meeting while offering nebulous and vague assessments to his face.

Either way, disappointment or praise, when that pooch looks up at you, so trusting, so wanting to please, so full of expectation—what do you do? You might say something like "Aw c'mon over here." And you love it up unconditionally.

That's the trick. It's as simple as the "L" word. Love. I always say unless you love your people unconditionally, you'll never hear the truth again. Oh, employees will talk to you, sure. But instead of telling you the truth you need, they'll tell you what they think you want to hear. They'll tell you precisely what you communicate to them by your actions that you're willing to hear. And as leaders, as managers—you need the *truth.* So if employees aren't telling it to you—look to yourself. Are *you* creating a safe environment, where they can feel unconditional acceptance—even love—when they tell you disappointing news? As Colin Powell once said, "The day soldiers stop bringing you their problems is the day you have stopped leading them. They have either lost confidence that you can help or concluded you do not care. Either case is a failure of leadership."

E: The second letter of the acronym is E for empowerment. I know it's a popular word, but it's popular because it's so powerful. Leaders need to empower others to act—not be a "check with" or a "wait for" in the chain of command. Let go! I always believe that life operates by paradox. What you often think is—really isn't. And what you think isn't—really is. And since it's people that we're dealing with and not machine tools, the advice stands in the business world as well as in life. The paradox is simply this: whatever you want, give it away. If you want trust, give it away. If you want control, give it away. If you want love, give it away. If you want power, give it away. I've seen the truth of this life paradox played out over and over and over again, even in the business realm.

Philosophy @ Work

While a relatively young service representative in the eastern United States, I made my living calling on major trucking fleets from Maine to Maryland. One of the more challenging areas was in metropolitan New Jersey and New York. One particular fleet was an extremely challenging customer with a very aggressive and hot-tempered service manager.

When I assumed the position, I was taken to this customer's job site by my predecessor, and in retrospect, he couldn't get out of there fast enough. Our company was paying over one million dollars a year in extraordinary goodwill settlements for product problems beyond the warranty period with this customer, and I was told that my prime objective would be to reduce that spend. My predecessor informed me this was his most challenging customer and most contentious relationship. He confided that he gave up trying to reduce the settlements because the battles were just too personally stressful for him.

As I walked into the shop and met "Vinny," he immediately escorted me to a failed engine. It had experienced significant damage due to some assembly errors, with intake valves installed in exhaust ports and vice versa. The engine was a few thousand miles beyond the warranty period.

My predecessor examined the engine, and his technical assessment was that it had suffered the damage due to an over speed condition (meaning the engine was operated at an abnormal rpm, which caused the valve contact within the cylinders and the extenuating damage and contamination). Vinny was livid. He climbed all over that assessment with profanity-laced aggression. He looked immediately at me and asked me my opinion. I calmly said to Vinny, "Well, even if over speed, it doesn't explain the valve installation errors, does it? What do you think we should do, Vinny?"

He paused, a bit of shock apparent in his expression. He nearly yelled his response. "You should replace the entire engine! We didn't get the value from it you promised!"

I considered this only a moment and then said, "I agree with you. I approve." He stood there likely a bit stunned. And we moved on to other topics.

Over the course of our three-year relationship in this role, Vinny became accustomed to making his recommendations in a similar manner. We'd discuss every issue. Sometimes, he would still be his normally aggressive and cantankerous self. But paradoxically, I found over that time that Vinny throttled his demands considerably, and our dealings became very reasonable. There were still product issues. There were still goodwill adjustments made. But during that time, the size of his trucking fleet increased and the total dollar amount of his goodwill adjustments went significantly downward.

When I left the position, Vinny held a special luncheon for me with the company owner. He proudly proclaimed I was the "best but the toughest rep he'd ever dealt with!" I chuckled and told him I was a "marshmallow—a very soft touch."

He countered and said, "No, Bill, you're tough. But you're fair."

As I have reflected on this over the years I believe there's a very important philosophical lesson to be learned. I did not try to control Vinny. But in giving him the liberty to feel trusted, empowered, and respected, he throttled and controlled himself much more effectively than I ever could have with a continual confrontational approach. Again it reaffirmed by belief in the paradoxes of life.

If you desire that employees act decisively, you must give away the power to make decisions. Don't hoard it. Give it to them! If you want to make all the decisions for them, you may as well hoard all the choices, too. Rather, enable your people to be their most powerful selves. If you want power, give that to them. They will surprise you with their impact.

And no, you can't completely delegate accountability. That rests ultimately with you, the leader. But even when you can give them responsibility and with it, accountability for their part of the deliverables you assign, the total roll-up of accountability still rests with you. That's why selecting team members you can trust is so critical. But I'll guarantee you this: if you don't give trust, you won't get it. So the second aspect of the four-letter acronym is critical to engaging employees by showing them you trust them with their shoulder at the wheel. And the paradox is that they will be so covetous of maintaining and sustaining that trust that you will engage their hearts, minds, and passions so much more than by merely trying to manage or control them.

A: The third letter of the LEAD acronym is for authenticity. This is all about you. And that's okay. This is one time that it really should be all about you—the authentic you. The you that comes home at night should be the same you that shows up each day in the workplace. The illusion of work-life balance—implying that you can have a balanced ledger of your work and your personal time—is wishful thinking. For example, there are a mere twenty-four hours in a day. You might sleep eight—lucky you, if you do. You will work, say, ten. That alone leaves a whole six hours to cram in all that sought-after personal life balance. Well, subtract eating and commuting, and voila, you're down to about four hours to squeeze in all that wonderfully elusive balance. I've made the point.

There is no such thing as the mythical 50/50 split. In fact, the best definition I've heard for work-life balance is this: Whatever you derive value and purpose from, put 100 percent of yourself, your true, authentic self into it. Whether that is home, the job, church, or family—when you're there—be present. Be authentically you and *be there.* Unless you're an amazing super human being, you can't be 100 percent in two places at once—so that means your balance is not really about math but more about being 100 percent authentically you wherever you are.

Bill George, in his book *True North*, terms this "an integrated life." I prefer to think of it as a meaningful life. I've often counseled young employees that if they can't be authentically who they are at work, maybe it's not the right place to work. Think of it this way, if you will: if you have to be one artificial person at work and another at home, the energy level that faking demands will create enormous stresses on your spirit. And those stresses are not only unhealthy but are energy robbers that steal important creativity and passion from your daily work. So both the business and the employee are being cheated. If it's true for employees at large, it's certainly true for leaders. And when you are not authentically you, when you are masquerading as a manager or some inauthentic person in the chain of command, you're robbing yourself of energy as well. The best gift you can give yourself as a leader is a loving tolerance of who you are, and importantly, a loving tolerance of who you are not. Employees will read this authenticity. They can smell phony a mile away. So, the third letter of the acronym, A for authenticity, is a gift not only to the employees whose hearts you'll touch but to yourself as well.

D: The final letter is D for development. Here I hearken back to Ralph Nader's premise—"The function of leadership is to produce more leaders, not more followers." If you want employees whose engagement skyrockets, show them you care. What's the old saying? "No one cares how much you know until they know how much you care." And care for employees is more than a good benefits plan. It's caring for them as human beings. It's showing concern for their professional and personal growth and well-being. It's about providing opportunities to stretch and to test themselves under the caring and watchful eye of a leader who has created a safe place for them to become (like the army says) all that they can be.

And by the way, it isn't about motivating employees. The truth is, I don't think we can motivate anyone. The root word of motivate is motive. And motives are internal. So as a leader, you don't control inward motives. You can inspire them, but you can't control them. So in the realm of employee development, don't expect all employees to have a long list of development courses or seminars they want to attend. And don't think you've fulfilled your role as leader by providing a listing in the company or division's learning plan either. Caring for and inspiring employees comes from knowing them.

Philosophy @ Work

I was actually a bit shocked to learn how my employee group was so impressed with the fact that I scheduled an informal breakfast, lunch, or snack session with each of them—all 485 in my last division—to get to know them. It took nearly my first six months on the job to manage that scheduling challenge, but it was well worth it. I only had one rule: my guest employees could not tell me about their job description in any detail. What I wanted to know was their story. Of course, some human resource types reading this might cringe at this—after all, we are told to not ask certain types of questions during job interviews, right? Well, I wasn't conducting a job interview. I was conducting a conversation. And I wanted to get to know each of the employees as people first.

It was an incredible experience for me. I learned of interests, hobbies, talents, and even some personal challenges that I might never known without those sessions. I became aware of the incredible diversity within the employee team, and that was an unexpected gain. Here's the paradox. This effort was for me to get to know them, but it was the employees who felt significant and appreciated by this simple act.

I gave them time. They gave me so much more. And recognizing the unique talents and strengths of individual employees came in handy when selecting team members for specific challenges or assignments. In my view, their unique way of relating to the challenge would very often yield better results in less time.

So there you have it. The trick to engaging employees? Love them. Empower them. Be authentic with them. And develop them. I created employee-led culture teams. Each team created a vision of a future state for our cultural journey around the elements we wanted to incorporate into our culture. These ten elements included communication, values, leadership, safety, people development, work-life balance, learning, diversity, change management, and quality. I refused to publish it or to make it a formal program. But I did require one thing from each team: Under no circumstances were they allowed to approach the cultural changes they wanted to invoke by referring to the employee engagement scores. No reference to scores. No attempt to improve scores. In short, *no scores!*

The paradox? At the end of year two, when we were required to complete the company's on-line employee opinion survey, our division had the highest employee engagement scores in the company. Over 90 percent highly engaged … 93 percent, to be precise. Of course, we won the Chairman's Award (received honorable mention after year one, by the way). But I refused to hang banners or signs. It was *not* about scores. It was about creating a culture where people felt valued, felt cared for, felt known. And I knew by doing that, the numbers would take care of themselves.

My Soft-Side Philosophical Nugget:

Why is the soft side the hardest part of employee engagement? We make it harder than it has to be when we put human engagement into the language of management versus the language of people. We keep score. We have processes. We've made it a program. And in so doing we have lost the human touch, which is truly what engages the human heart. Lennon and McCartney had it right. You can't buy love. And you can't manage it, either. You can only lead people with caring, with heart, and by revealing to them the authentic you. When you do that, you will create a culture where they'll give you all they've got to give. And the results will speak volumes.

Chapter 5: Who'll Stop the Rain?

Long as I remember the rain's been comin' down.
Clouds of mystery pourin' confusion on the ground.
Good men through the ages, tryin' to find the sun;
And I wonder, still I wonder, who'll stop the rain.
I went down Virginia, seekin' shelter from the storm.
Caught up in the fable, I watched the tower grow.
Five-year plans and new deals, wrapped in golden chains.
And I wonder, still I wonder who'll stop the rain.
Heard the singers playin', how we cheered for more.
The crowd had rushed together, tryin' to keep warm.
Still the rain kept pourin', fallin' on my ears.
And I wonder, still I wonder who'll stop the rain.
Words and Music by John Fogerty (1978)

So many movements in the business world have tried to find the sun—or metaphorically stated, have strained to burst through the weeds to find the light of day, struggling to bud into the next great silver bullet and to bloom as an antidote for ailing business performance. These movements take root in the boardrooms and executive offices of corporations, and they are chisel-plowed and seeded into underfertilized fields of skeptical employees, the same employees who time and again have endured the forced cultivation of yet another crop of ideas ballyhooed as the new sure-fire answer to all that ails business.

In the course of nearly thirty years in the corporate world, I saw this time and again with programs like Total Quality Management, ISO 9000, and Oliver Wight's Class A certification program. There were also well-intended efforts like customer satisfaction survey programs, which were then trumped by customer loyalty measurement programs. And most recently, manufacturing firms have eagerly embraced the much-venerated Toyota Production System. In my experience, we'd go all out with intense bursts of activity and training initially. But these efforts would soon give way to the next great hope, a new program. Rarely did any of these initiatives stand for long.

But on and on these programs are paraded as a continual deluge of concepts, programs, ideologies, and theories—all purported to be the magic pill, the next great hope for business. And all are unleashed on weary and wary employees who have earned their cynicism honestly and who are tired of enduring yet another "flavor of the month" concept in a flood of varieties that would easily eclipse Baskin Robbins. But never before had I witnessed anything so fervently embraced and zealously pushed as the religion of 6 Sigma.

I say religion because in my experience, it was deemed almost sacred. Employees were indoctrinated in the mantra, the "apostle's creed" of 6 Sigma philosophy. And it was replete with a compliance-based liturgy—even to the point that upon its initial rollout, all executives were required to stand front-and-center before the CEO (who wore a traditional karate robe) to recite their "elevator speech" supporting the cult leader's new vision. The Kool-Aid was passed around, and everyone apparently sipped willingly—if not mindlessly. In reality, they merely complied. But as British statesman John Morley once said, "You have not converted a man merely because you have silenced him."

What bothered me most about the implementation approach in my company was its compliance bias. I kept remembering what Gary Hamel of the London School of Business said about process conformance. He argues that diligence, compliance, and conformance to process are commodities, and that innovation, passion, and creativity are the only true differentiators in the twenty-first century. The well-intended CEO at the time launched a rigorous rollout—executed extremely faithfully by the duly appointed lead zealot, a.k.a. "Corporate Deployment Champion." I worried then and am convinced now that my skepticism was well founded. It's not processes that are the problem, by the way. It's the unintended consequence of a process focus that can actually impede employees from doing truly extraordinary things. We must be careful not to mire them in a bog of rules and procedures that may stifle their unique ingenuity—ingenuity that can often lead to extraordinary solutions and outstanding results.

Time and again I took note that overreliance on technique and prescribed process ignored the reality that processes don't delight customers; people do. I've heard it said that 95 percent of the time when customers are delighted, it is because an employee either felt empowered or risked stepping beyond process to deal intelligently with a situation involving an exception overlooked by prescribed methodologies. I believe what author Clay Shirky wrote, that process "is an embedded reaction to prior stupidity." Checks and balances are important, but too much bureaucracy can kill risk taking.

Processes—as all-encompassing as they strive to be—are recipes of steps to follow in anticipation of all possible scenarios, and they are typically codified and solidified as new process modifications only when we learn from some prior mistake or when an unanticipated exception bites us. It's only then that we recognize the prior prescription didn't consider quite everything. In those decisive moments, what writer and business leader Jan Carlzon calls those "moments of truth," when employees don't have a "bible" of process for reference, what does an employee do? When the process fails to address the situation, what should an employee say? "I'm sorry, Mr. Customer, my script doesn't address this contingency?" Clearly not.

Oh sure, processes are important, but not to the exclusion of an overarching philosophy of empowering people to "do the right thing." One element of a business culture that must be carved out or preserved as a "trump card" to process conformance is empowerment given to employees to do the right thing in those moments of truth. They must be liberated to go beyond the recipe. Leadership embraces this ambiguity and empowers people to respond accordingly. Managers merely play it safe and follow the rules. The paradox is that by playing it safe, they actually put the business at more risk of disappointing those customers they are endeavoring to serve.

Businesses today seem to have such a process bias, especially in larger companies, that they stifle employee innovation. But it invariably comes down to this: what differentiates a company is its people. The rules don't rule. The passion and commitment of people rule the day. You cannot legislate behavior. Just look at any religion for confirmation of that truth. The rules exist, but they don't control behavior. They merely guide it. It comes down to individual choice. As Teddy Roosevelt said, "In any moment of decision the best thing you can do is the right thing. The next best thing you can do is the wrong thing. The worst thing you can do is nothing." When a company lays out its rules of engagement, it must be careful to avoid stripping employees of their liberty to employ their own ingenuity and passion to solve problems.

I also fear that there are other pitfalls for the people side of business through overreliance on process. Let's go back to 1913 when Henry Ford implemented the automobile assembly line. Two things he focused on were efficiency of throughput and output volume. Frederic Taylor is credited with inventing the assembly-line approach, and he once quipped, "People are merely parts of an assembly line. You don't spend time motivating them anymore than you spend time motivating a drill press." Pretty inspiring, huh? Taylor apparently believed that people needed to think less about the work they did, and become a "tool"—an "instrument to do work" as a part of the process. True, the work was likely less creative and more systematic: repetitive motion, repetitive tasks, no need for ingenuity; just follow the procedures. But if you think about your grandfather or great-grandfather, he more likely was a craftsman. He had an absolute linkage between his human ingenuity and his physical act of labor to create his product, whether that was furniture making or construction.

Similarly when businesses today focus on repetitively performed tasks per the prescribed process, the implicit premise is that you can separate the need for human ingenuity from the physical act of labor. Even if that labor is the work of thinking. Is the overreliance on 6 Sigma and process, technique, and systems risking the isolation of human ingenuity from our work? It seems to me it could be doing precisely that. The implication is that the output is assured if you follow the process repetitively, if not mindlessly. That might work in many situations, but it is not a cure-all. In those moments of truth, I prefer to rely on intelligent human choice over process any day.

Philosophy @ Work

I once had a difficult issue spanning three divisions, and the competing priorities of our various interests were tripping up our respective teams as they attempted to derive a compromise solution. After about three months of stymied action, the issue was elevated to me. I simply called my counterparts and suggested the three of us meet over lunch to achieve consensus on a go-forward strategy. I felt that if we could remove the clutter of our divisional self-interests, we could liberate out teams to think outside the proverbial box and come up with the best solution, and I was certainly willing to take the risk that might involve compromise on my part.

One peer agreed readily, and we synched calendars. The other peer agreed conceptually with the need but suggested that he'd check his calendar and get back with us. Two days later, I received an e-mail from him, which merely forwarded a 6 Sigma project charter to "guide our conversation." Frankly, I was incredulous. Our teams were struggling to get beyond their own loyalty to divisional priorities while following a process map, and here we were, the leaders of the groups, about to commission a project charter to guide a simple conversation? I was appalled at the attempted deflection of genuine dialogue.

I called the peer involved and challenged his approach, stating simply, "We don't need a process map to guide an open conversation. Let's just meet and chat. I'm sure we can come to a clear consensus." Again, to my alarm, my peer said impishly, "I thought 6 Sigma was the way we worked." This was an obvious and transparent reference to our corporate strategy document, which claimed that we would, in fact, work utilizing the "facts and data" principles of 6 Sigma. In my mind, however, this peer was hiding behind process and had apparently lost the courage, if not the will, to speak openly, honestly, and vulnerably about the problem without the umbrella of process to protect his interests. I called off the meeting. The project languished for three more months. It only moved forward when this individual was transferred.

We ignore to our peril that human ingenuity has an inextricable link to work. It is not about mindlessly following process. Differentiation today, as Hamel suggests, is about linking human passion, ingenuity, creativity, and innovation to our work. I fear that process zeal is becoming an American business disease right now. I think that what made American entrepreneurialism so great was innovation and risk taking, not following process. Sometimes you risk and win. Sometimes you risk and lose. But not all things in the world are empirical. Sometimes, leaders must have the courage to bridge the faith gap between empirical analysis and acting with urgency by trusting their character and instincts.

There is another concern I feel that springs from too rigorously holding onto prescribed processes as the magic bullet for all business problems. As young employees come on stream, I fear that we're creating a very tentative cadre of talented people who are gaining this tentativeness as another unintended consequence of 6 Sigma. We're teaching or implying that business success comes from being "jointly and severally responsible." We are teaching them that it's all about "facts and data." There is precious little certainty in this world, especially in today's rapidly changing business environment.

I read an article recently about the "Delusion of Certainty" by Phil Rosenzweig. All things in life are relative, he argues, including decisions. We make choices and dare to presume that competition is sitting still. Good decisions may turn out bad. Bad decisions may turn out good.

Philosophy @ Work

Let me share a personal story with you about an on-highway trucker that changed my life—a southern boy who operated an eighteen-wheeler as an owner-operator. When I was a young employee in my firm back in 1980, I barely had a year under my belt and yet was assigned to a developmental pre-field position in our service department on the customer contact desk. Due to my lack of seniority, I was on that desk during the forced summer vacation shutdown period. I was alone and on my own, and I received a phone call from an irate trucking customer. His name was Mr. Ranny Davis from Mississippi. His truck engine had just failed in a disastrous way. He had just shucked a connecting rod through his engine block, destroying the engine. He was madder than a hornet—cursing, railing at product quality, demanding that I replace his engine.

I really did not know what to do—the engine repair would have cost eighteen thousand dollars. The engine replacement would have cost twenty thousand dollars. I spoke to the local repair center's service manager and asked his opinion. He confirmed the engine damage and recommended that I replace the engine. He admitted, "If it was my engine, I'd want you to replace it." So, with nothing more than that bit of reflection, I authorized it. At the time, being quite junior on the desk, I had a whopping fifteen hundred dollar claims authority limit. What was I thinking making a twenty thousand dollar decision? But it felt right.

When my boss returned from vacation, let's just say I received coaching. Notably, I did not get killed. I learned, but I wasn't punished. I remember thinking, "That's the worst thing I could have done—but it's all I knew to do." From that point, I knew something else about asking the right questions before I leapt into action. But I was never criticized for making the decision, only for my decision-making thought process. But the important lesson was this: it didn't stop me from being willing to leap into the deep end of the ocean. My manager gave me some better floaties so I could swim a bit safer next time. But that's the worst thing that happened. I grew. I swam stronger and smarter into the next wave.

Now, let's fast forward. It's twenty years later, and I am the worldwide general manager for Caterpillar's on-highway engine business. I was attending a customer-marketing event, and one of the visitor service reps said, "Some guy is desperate to meet you." I reluctantly said, "Bring him over"—not knowing what I was getting into.

A man came up to me beaming and said in a heavy southern drawl, "Are you Bill Mayo? You may not remember me, but twenty years ago you replaced my engine. And you never even asked me if my fuel rack was jacked up—and it was. Since then, I've become the VP of sales for Empire Truck Sales in Meridian, Mississippi. And because of you, I've sold a runnin' ton of your product. I just wanted to thank you, man!" I still carry his business card today.

There are two important lessons from this story. One is the obvious lesson to do the right thing, as best you know it to be; but if you err, err on the side of the customer. The other lesson comes from my supervisor's reaction to my mistake. He did not criticize my motives for taking care of the customer. He looked at intent and guided me with the wisdom of his experience to ensure that my decision-making process for the future was better informed. He helped me to grow and to learn. He also never questioned my assumption of a twenty thousand dollar authority limit, even though I had only a fifteen hundred dollar limit. Not once did that topic ever come up. He was interested in teaching, not scolding. And his courage to let me wander way beyond my process-imposed limits encouraged me, inspired me, and built trust and confidence. From that manager I learned that I could gain authority by taking decisive action. And he was pleased with that initiative, finding the golden nugget in my motives.

My Soft-Side Philosophical Nugget:

Why is the soft side the hardest part of processes? We make it harder than it has to be when we ignore the power of human ingenuity, creativity, and passion. These are the key differentiators for business, for solving problems, and for delighting customers. The overriding philosophy must be to empower people to "do the right thing." Clearly there are risks involved in granting that liberty, but there is a greater peril involved in too much reliance on process. As certain as I am that it all comes down to people, I'm also certain that the flood of prescriptive solutions will continue to deluge businesses today. Leaders must stop the rain of prescriptive management control and be risk takers to tap into the passions of people. Only then can we assure that our businesses will not only stay afloat amid the torrential downpour of new imagined silver bullets but that the results achieved will be well beyond the scripted outcomes we presume that process will assure on their own.

Chapter 6: Upside Down

Upside down
Boy you turn me
Inside out
And round and round
Words and Music by Nile Rodgers and Bernard Edwards (1980)

Upside down. Inside out. Round and round. Am I talking about business management? Unfortunately, yes! An esteemed colleague of mine, Dr. Michael J. O'Connor, terms it "managing backward." What he's referring to flips traditional management practices on their side—or perhaps, upside down. Mike bases his argument on a body of research spanning over thirty years. As founder of the Center for Managing by Values, Mike suggests that sluggish business performance in most companies is rarely the fault of shifting markets, stiff competition, or lack of resources. The truth is rather that most organizations don't manage their business priorities in the proper order to actually shape sustained success.

For example, think about the typical management of companies—let's say the company you currently work for or have worked for. What were their execution priorities? How did they manage something such as bringing a new idea or new product or service to market? O'Connor's research suggests that the norm is to first develop a strategy and tactics to implement the plan. Most often, what follows is significant effort to define required systems and processes to support implementation and to track performance. From this point, organizational structure considerations are addressed. Who does what? Who reports to whom? Who will manage the implementation? Who are the "feet on the street" responsible to sell the product? Obviously, in this phase, people are considered, of course. But typically, that focus is limited to identifying bodies and the required training necessary to make the sales people successful in meeting sales targets. O'Connor's research identifies that only very rarely is the element of culture addressed, nor is how the product or service aligns with the company's cultural values.

Mike argues, "They have it backward." Although admittedly, a business can indeed get short bursts of productivity or performance improvement in this manner, the research confirms that a sustained track record of success over the long-term requires a preeminent focus on culture and people *first!* As author Jim Collins suggests in his famous books *Good to Great* and *Built to Last*, companies today must focus on building a winning culture first.

Author and consultant Peter Drucker is credited with the popular sentiment, "Management is about doing things right; leadership is doing right things." While this makes for a great comparative mantra, it's a bit too simplistic in my view. In business, at least the last time I checked, both are required—doing things right and doing right things. In the example above, the implementation of a new product or service, clearly there is a need for implementation plans to be executed in the right way. While culture is a leadership-shaped phenomenon, Collins' and O'Connor's work suggests that building a winning culture is far too often ignored and that management priorities typically have it backward. Why? Why do businesses today get tripped up and ignore the leadership imperative to build culture? Why is there a backward focus from management to the obvious linkage of culture and people to sustained performance success? Indeed, it seems to be upside down, turned around, and inside out. Why?

This is a complex question to answer without generalizations. Each business is different, of course. But, I generally do believe there is an overemphasis on management and underdevelopment of leadership in the typical business culture. Management seeks compliance. I can't tell you how many businessmen and women I've met who have lamented in confidence their firm was "over-managed and under-led."

Perhaps one of the main reasons for that perception is rooted simply in the distinction between what managers do and what leaders do. Management focuses on control, and things like strategy, systems, processes, and employee training naturally follow. Management wants to rein things in. After all, managers are charged with execution of the plan, and they want to ensure achievement of expected results. Management is defined in Webster's as "the process of dealing with and *controlling* people or things." And that's the culture that employees feel. Interestingly, the word's etymological origins suggest it comes from the Italian word *maneggiare*, which relates to handling a horse!

Leadership is more about letting go. A leader is defined simply as "someone people follow." Most employees do not sense this level of empowerment in the work environment; hence, to them, the culture is "over-managed" and "under-led."

So why do managers appear to their employees as reluctant to lead? This whole leadership thing can be scary stuff, precisely because it is not about control. Leadership is about *inspiration* such that people willingly follow you. When you're in control, you feel more powerful, safer, more in charge of your own destiny, if you will. When you're leading, you surrender control via the faith you're placing in others. It can make you feel vulnerable.

> ***Philosophy @ Work***
>
> *There is a scene in the film Dead Poets Society where an eccentric teacher, played by Robin Williams, leads his male students into the hallway to view a trophy case. As he encourages them to lean in to really see the athletes in the sepia-tone photographs of old sports teams, he whispers in their ears, "Carpe Diem, boys. Seize the day. Make your lives extraordinary."*
>
> *When I arrived at my new position as vice president of Caterpillar's North American marketing unit, I inherited an outstanding and top-performing team. I was an outsider, an unknown, but I was coming into the largest, most profitable division of the marketing world, and the twelve department managers were no doubt a bit anxious about how I might change things.*
>
> *In one of my first meetings with my direct reports, I took a very vulnerable risk. Parroting Robin Williams, I stood on a chair and recited the lines to "Oh Captain, My Captain," just as Williams' character did in the film. I invited them to join me in "seizing the day." I told them that I would honor the past and their outstanding record of achievement but that I did not come to manage the status quo. I invited them to put their thumbprints on this place—to leave their legacy and build an even better culture and record of achievement for those that would follow us.*
>
> *I explained to them that we would put people first. We would embark upon a cultural journey, engaging our people in its creation, and from that, all good results would follow. I asked*

them to have faith. I invited them not a journey of managing the division, but a journey of leading the division to a better place. And I invited them to take my hand and come with me to that better place.

I'm sure there were more than a few arched eyebrows at this somewhat eccentric call to action. But in the months that followed, they believed. This team reconstructed all department meetings, saving countless hours and eliminating meetings that were merely perfunctory. They reconstructed and simplified our overly complex business metrics. They created a "blue dot" vision for where we wanted to be and where we wanted to lead our dealers into the future. And notably, this team and our employees turned the tide on three years of successive market share erosion in our core products. This leadership team, which had, by the way, previously been called the "admin team" engaged in a cultural transformation with me that in two years time resulted in the highest levels of employee engagement of all marketing units in the company.

I invited them to give me their hearts. And they did. And I empowered them to make the differences they wanted to make to improve our culture, our business, and our team. Unleashing their potential and seeing it manifest into truly notable results was one of the most gratifying experiences of my career.

A business essentially wants to control risk and assure outcomes. It attempts to do this with controls. It attempts to control its products, its markets, its distribution, its manufacturing processes, *and* its people. Clearly those who achieve success as managers are those who have demonstrated a consistent track record of meeting those outcomes while mitigating those pesky risks. One merely needs to look to the chain of command to realize that those higher up in the organization are typically those who have risen through the ranks by minimizing adverse impacts of all those threatening risks associated with running a business.

Having said that, I don't mean to trivialize management's importance. Management is a critical element of business to be sure. You cannot run a successful business without an appropriate level of controls. But leadership unleashes people to achieve beyond the controls. While following a management approach may have the illusion of safety, my point is simply that management control will not yield the most dramatic results; leadership does that.

But leadership feels much more risky. As a leader you are certain about your vision—what *needs to happen*—but less sure about the "how tos" that assure the outcome.

And yet, true leaders do exist. They set the vision for their team, set an example of trust and integrity, and establish a sense of community among team members. They actually rely much more upon faith that people will rise to great levels of achievement simply by being empowered to do the right thing in support of the desired state. Leaders achieve these results not by controlling people but by inspiring them. And this approach sets the tone for the entire culture of the organization.

A leader relies upon others to perform in the face of stress, pressure, or risks. This may create a very genuine sense of fear and vulnerability. Who would want to lead when there is such a genuine ambiguity associated with the assurance of outcome? It's much easier to manage assets. But as I've argued previously, people are *not* assets. I certainly would not want to work in a culture that boasted, "People are our most important depreciable work tool!" Yet many companies implicitly boast just that by declaring people are their most important assets.

Paradoxically, "management control" somewhat implies an approach that views people as instruments to do work. In my mind, this actually stifles true empowerment and creativity. Managers can be rigid, often seeking the safety of conformance and compliance with processes to achieve the desired end, whereas leadership is nimble, granting empowerment and liberty to achieve the desired end. Management overemphasizes coloring within the lines; but true breakthroughs come at the boundaries and beyond the boundaries. And perhaps even more important, excessive human control creates emotional disengagement among employees.

People want to feel that their role actually supports a greater vision. As we've discussed previously, they want to be a part of something more noble and bigger than themselves. They don't want to merely comply; they want to matter. For an authentic leader, people will put self beneath team. They will be less concerned about their limited authority and tightly defined roles, and they will be more concerned about overall team performance.

Importantly, the business vision—that "noble purpose"—is what reigns supreme, not the position of the manager. In short, everyone leads. Everyone gives their heart, their discretionary and emotional commitment, beyond their obligatory compliance. And everyone is committed to the noble purpose inspired by the leader. In my mind, this is much more powerful and, dare I say, *more fun*! It will also yield much greater results. But this approach feels a bit "out there" and a trifle too risky for the young leader. And it may even feel risky for the business. Therefore, in my view, businesses typically don't create this type of environment, and few managers are willing to work on the ragged edge or perimeter of the prevailing culture.

So yes, I generally believe that businesses create cultures that groom more managers than leaders. By being overwhelmingly concerned with controls, they are naturally less concerned with liberating their leaders *or* their employees. Paradoxically, businesses reap what they sow. Management cultures breed more managers. When businesses sow management control as the pervasive philosophy, they will reap a compliant and conforming culture among its employees. While performance of the business might be good, as Jim Collins urged us all, we should strive to stretch beyond good to great, beyond great to greater.

Tom Peters once said, "All progress is made by people who get pissed off." While I understand that he was speaking not of anger but of discontent with the status quo, I don't think discontent is the secret sauce. I believe true progress comes through inspiration. And that's where a leader plays his or her most important and game-changing role.

While I acknowledge that both management and leadership are required, I am concerned about people being choked and smothered by a fog of irrelevant and stifling controls. At the end of the day, business isn't brain surgery. It's about producing value in a product and by providing a valuable service at a competitive price. Running the business efficiently rewards the company with profit for the effort.

I've often heard that I seem to be over the top in attributing great significance to a people-oriented culture in order for leadership and business results to flourish. Of that, I am guilty as charged. But I believe this expressed concern often masks a more challenging question. How do you address peers or superiors who do not buy in to the people or soft side of business; those who rely more upon a command-and-control approach to accomplish results?

Philosophy @ Work

With the number of assignments I had over the course of a long career, it was inevitable that my philosophy and that of a boss or other colleague might clash once in a while. In my most recent assignment, there was one particular peer who was a thorn in my side, as I was in his. I used to work for him and then was promoted to peer level. Our roles interfaced. It was awkward and apparent to our teams that we had different views, different philosophies, and very different leadership styles. To be candid, I heard on a number of occasions hearsay about negative comments he had made regarding me. And I was not immune to the temptation to retaliate and speak ill of him. And to my shame, I did on occasion, borne of frustration.

Naturally, this spilled over into our collaboration, and our teams were torn between competing loyalties. One day, following a daylong officer-level meeting, I asked to speak with him privately. We headed to my office, and I spoke these words (I'll refer to him as Joe, obviously not his real name): "Joe, thanks for coming. What I'm about to say needed to be said months ago. We obviously have very different perspectives, and I'll admit I have a problem with your approach and attitude. But the truth is, as the Bible says, 'As much as it lies within me, I must strive to live at peace with all men.' So Joe, I won't go into any defense of my attitude or actions or things you may have heard attributed to me. What I am asking you for today is something we don't often hear in the world of business. I am asking for your forgiveness. I am sorry for my part, and I pledge that I will not vilify you in any way from this point forward. Our teams must work together. We must work together. I ask you for forgiveness for my part of the problem, and I am sorry."

He sat there in silence for a moment and finally said, "Well, you have had a problem with me, and I have had a problem with you. But I accept your apology."

> *We shook hands, and he departed. I could not believe that he didn't reciprocate, but it wasn't offered as a quid pro quo. I knew that I must strive to live at peace with all men, Joe included. And although I did not respect this manager's approach, he deserved my cooperation and good will. From that point forward, we "made nice" publicly, put our teams to work on a number of collaborative projects, and slowly started to turn around some pesky problem areas between our divisions. I was disappointed in his reaction, but I rationalized that I am only accountable for mine.*

Generally speaking, when I encountered a colleague or boss who was overly prescriptive or controlling with regard to either me or other employees, I couldn't keep silent. I simply tried to model my authentic behaviors, speak my authentic values, coach in an authentic way, and discuss points of disagreement openly. But frankly, if the manager was not dissuaded from his or her approach, I did the best I could to produce results by leading my team authentically and by letting the results speak for themselves.

I did not rely upon all the red/yellow/green metrics charts. I was very selective and gave my team permission to say "no" to certain imposed initiatives. We quite frankly could not chase all the programs and initiatives emanating from corporate. I consistently attempted to provide a buffer for my team when upper-management criticism became overly focused on those colored metric charts. This took a lot of courage on my part and a lot of faith on the part of my team. I held that task as one of my highest accountabilities, to ensure their safety for loyally following my lead.

I led my team by setting a vision, by setting an example, and by creating a sense of community. I did not chase metrics. If necessary, I would be open with my team about any disconnect with management without sounding disloyal. I have always admonished myself, as well as others, to find something to emulate about every manager you work for and something to forgive—forgive being the operative word, because we're all flawed human beings. I am certain that despite my best intentions, I will disappoint someone sometime. Yet I am just as convinced that there is good in everyone, and disagreements do not have to mean disloyalty.

My Soft-Side Philosophical Nugget:

Why is the soft side so hard when it comes to executing business priorities? We make it harder than it has to be when we execute our priorities backward. Businesses today risk getting out of balance between controlling and liberating people. Employees and culture must *come first. Everything else follows. An organization's culture is shaped by its leaders. A people-oriented culture must exist for leaders to thrive throughout the organization, because again, people are not assets. I'm convinced that you can get human performance through management, just not the best performance. Just as I'm convinced you can't lead a drill press; you can only manage it. You can lead an emotional human being because you can inspire. You can touch the human heart. You can connect people to a vision worthy of their emotional commitment, their discretionary effort. And this will liberate their true and greatest potential. That's where true breakthroughs and outstanding results will come from.*

Chapter 7: I Love You Just the Way You Are

Don't go changing, to try and please me
You never let me down before
Don't imagine you're too familiar
And I don't see you anymore
I wouldn't leave you in times of trouble
We never could have come this far
I took the good times, I'll take the bad times
I'll take you just the way you are
Words and Music by Billy Joel (1977)

The popular film *Nanny Diaries* starring Scarlett Johansson is the story of her character's journey as she struggles to understand her place in the world. In one poignant scene, her character, Annie Braddock, a young woman from a working-class New Jersey neighborhood, attends a job interview with a prestigious firm. The interviewer begins with a warm, engaging smile and asks a seemingly benign and simple question: "Who is Annie Braddock?" Easy enough, but Annie chokes. Her angst is reflected by her numerous false starts, aborted answers, and obvious discomfort with the question. She eventually manages to blurt out an all-too-common admission. "I have no idea!" she declares and abruptly exits the office. Interview over!

Who am I really? That is the fundamental question each aspiring leader must answer with deep personal reflection. As Warren Bennis once said, "Leadership is a function of knowing yourself."

Paris-born author and physician Somerset Maugham said, "There are three rules for creating good leaders. Unfortunately, no one knows what they are!" That puts the words of this chapter in their proper context. They aren't rules. More importantly, they certainly aren't *the* rules. They're more aptly termed life lessons; lessons I've been privileged (sometimes painfully forced) to learn. To a great degree, it's impossible to separate my life philosophy from my leadership philosophy. But if, as Somerset Maugham suggests, there indeed are three rules for creating good leaders, I'm going to list my three and explain how I attempt to live them.

I've referenced Ralph Nader's admonition that claims that a key function of leadership is to create more leaders. Clearly, the impact that this renowned attorney and consumer rights activist has had on the world of business was not done in isolation. It required the recruitment and development of countless co-leaders. You might remember him for his key role in the creation of the EPA, OSHA, and the Freedom of Information Act— perhaps not the type of business leadership you might expect me to reference, but his impact is undeniable. And he most certainly developed a number of leaders to carry on that work. I agree with his sentiment, by the way. Leadership is not about creating followers. The number-one duty of a leader is to build the next generation of leaders.

> **Philosophy @ Work**
>
> *I remember leading a seminar where I suggested that no one in that sophisticated audience would blindly follow me merely because I was the conference leader. Sure enough, I asked them, "If I told you stand up right now, would you do it?" To a person, the audience remained seated. There was the obvious awkwardness and discomfort, as they were not expecting this at all. Then I added, "What if I told you that there was a silver dollar taped under ten random seats in this meeting room. Would you stand up to look now?" Predictably, after a short period of evaluation and skepticism, their internal motivations took over. First one, then five, and finally the entire room stood up and excitedly looked under their chairs. And as I promised, beneath ten seats were taped silver dollars, special silver dollars engraved with Dwight Eisenhower's likeness. I use Eisenhower dollars to illustrate our thirty-fourth president's insightful quote about leadership: "Leadership is getting other people to do what you want done because they want to do it."*
>
> *This lesson was used time and again as I attempted to lead by communicating my vision in a manner that could be internalized and related to benefits not only for the business but for the employees as well.*

A leader must paint a vision that inspires others to act. A leader must touch people's hearts and let them know that there's a better place out there, a place of value, something worth aspiring to. Rarely, by the way, does that better place involve money. In fact, I would argue that it's *never* about money, but it is about touching every individual with a vision that paints something of value. A vision must tap into that favorite radio station we all dial into … WII-FM (What's in it for me?).

Another great president, Abraham Lincoln, once said, "Nearly any man can stand adversity; if you really want to test his character, give him power." Lincoln understood that positions of leadership carry great power. But power can corrupt man's best intentions. You might be familiar with British Lord John Acton's famous nineteenth-century statement, "Power tends to corrupt. Absolute power corrupts absolutely."

Leadership is *not* about power. It's not about position, authority, or being at the top of a hierarchy; leadership is really all about service.

Here is my favorite personal quote about leadership and indeed about life. Nobel Prize winner and missionary Albert Schweitzer, who was also a physician, humanitarian, and most notably a philosopher, offers this wonderful perspective. It is one that I believe has great relevance for business and leadership: "I know not what your destiny will be, but this one thing I know. Those among you who have sought and found how to *serve* will truly be happy." This is the whole duty, privilege, and joy of leadership.

So what is a leader's job? How does a leader serve his or her organization and the people that comprise it? Quite simply, in my view, it is to do three things: set the vision, set the example, and create a sense of community. That's it. These are my version of Somerset Maugham's three rules. The next logical question you might have is "How does one do that?" And I'd like to suggest that it's not really that complicated. Just two things: know yourself, and be yourself. Every leader must be authentically who he or she is. People easily detect imposters and simply will not follow them. They might comply, but they will never give their heart to someone they do not have faith in.

To be an authentic leader, you simply have to know what you stand for. You must deeply know yourself. You must lead and live by a set of personal credos. I'm going to share mine, but with two caveats. First, it really doesn't matter what mine are. My credos work for me. But it matters very much what *yours* are. I'm only going to review mine as a thought provoker. I truly believe that each leader who is serious about developing a personal leadership philosophy should do this same exercise and write their personal values or credos. Once written, share them with your team. Hold yourself, and allow them to hold you, accountable for living and leading with them. Frankly, it takes a tremendous amount of personal reflection to develop your values statements. It takes even more effort to live them.

The second caveat is this: while I believe in these credos, I'm simply a human being, and one thing I can say with certainty being human is that I know that at some point in time I will disappoint others, even those I'm privileged to be leading. With those disclaimers out of the way, I'll begin. These ten credos reflect my personal leadership philosophy and will help illustrate what has shaped my personal approach to leading people. I've already shared three. Number one: **People are not assets.** Number two: **Strive to treat people like dogs**. And number three: **One cannot motivate others.**

As a quick recap, what is an asset? A thing, a machine tool, for example. And businesses use assets, consume them, and write them off and discard them when they have used up their value. Not a very soft-side approach, is it? As for recapping the credo of Striving to Treat People Like Dogs, it simply comes down to this: We treat dogs better than people! We provide clear expectations, immediate feedback, be it praise or constructive feedback for improvement, and unconditional love and acceptance. And as for motivation, that is an internal force. A leader can only inspire. People motivate themselves. So what about the others on my list? Here they are, in no particular order, with an explanation for each.

Number four: Sift the Nuggets. There is an excellent book entitled *The Power of Simplicity—A Management Guide to Cutting Through the Nonsense and Doing Things Right* by Jack Trout. I read it several years ago and was struck by one particular statistic.

When Shakespeare wrote Hamlet in 1601, the English language had about 20 thousand total words. Almost 262 years later, when Lincoln penned the Gettysburg address, the language had swollen to about 60 thousand words. At the time Trout wrote the book, estimates were that the English language had again ballooned to over 600 thousand words. Today, by the way, estimates are 989 thousand! Now reflect with me for a moment on the e-mails you receive in your workplace. How many of them are crisp, clear, and succinct? Sometimes, I think we try to fill business e-mails with as many hundred-dollar words as we can to make it sound professional or important. My leadership advice? *Keep it simple!* Remember George Bernard Shaw's quote: "The great illusion with communication is thinking it has taken place!"

Let's try an experiment from Trout's text. He offers these clever examples. What does this phrase mean? "It is not efficacious to indoctrinate a super-annuated canine with innovative maneuvers." What's it saying? Simply said, it means you can't teach old dog new tricks! Or how about this one? "Visible vapors emanating from carbonaceous materials are a harbinger of imminent conflagration." Simple, right? Wouldn't it be better to simply say, "Where there's smoke there's fire?"

As a leader, we need to keep our communications simple. Again, think of touching people's hearts, not making their eyes go glassy by attempting to be a verbose elocutionist—I mean, a wordy speaker!

Number 5: Let the Mutants Dance. This is all about the freedom to fail and to take risks, or as Norman Schwarzkopf termed it, the latitude to learn.

Do you know anything about honeybees? They apparently fly to and from a source of nectar in a straight line, a triangular formation, but in a straight line. That's where we get the phrase beeline. Apparently, bees can transmit a sound or frequency to other bees that communicates direction and distance to the source. It's called their waggle dance. And most all bees can interpret the dance and join in the formation and beeline it straight to and from the source of nectar.

However, entomologists say that 18 percent of bees are genetic mutants and apparently can't follow these directions. As a result, they wander off onto other directions, other paths. But guess what? Doing so actually ensures the survival of the colony! Without these mutants venturing off in other directions, the other bees would simply fly to and fro in a straight line until they exhausted the source of nectar necessary for the production of honey for the colony. In other words, thank God for the mutants! We, as leaders, have to allow space for the worker bees to take these other directions, to take risks, to learn other ways of doing things. If not, we risk extinction.

Number 6: There's no traffic jam in the extra mile. This is something I can still hear my father saying, and even in the Bible it says if a man asks you to walk a mile with him, go with him two. Essentially, I look for this in people. Not just those who do the required work, but those who go the extra mile. And I try to provide an example of that in my own work habits. I remember getting a call about 7 PM on a Friday night from a dealer manager early in my field career. I answered the phone in my home office, and his first words were, "I *knew* I could count on you!" The paradox was that this little vote of confidence spurred me on to ensure that I was always there in the extra mile lane.

Number 7: Be quick to hear and slow to speak. My dad actually said it more simply. He made a plaster plaque that yet hangs on my wall today. It says, "Oh Lord, help me to keep my big mouth shut." A critical job of a leader is to listen, not to talk. You have two ears and only one mouth. In my mind, you should use them in direct proportion, about twice as much listening as talking. Besides, and I don't know who actually said this, "When I'm talking, I'm not learning anything." A key role of leadership is to learn, *not* just to teach. Rock legend Jimi Hendrix said it best: "Knowledge speaks, wisdom listens."

Number 8: Do good versus look good. And here, I will offer a quote from an unlikely source for business wisdom, Mother Teresa. She once said, "The good you do today will often be forgotten tomorrow. Do good anyway." And it is the doing that matters—not the looking. There's a great cartoon that illustrates the point to look beneath the surface beyond the obvious appearance. It illustrates a lovely and shapely bikini-clad beauty standing off shore in water up to her neck. Standing near her is a handsome stranger; at least he's handsome on the surface. But beneath the water line, he's a short, pot-bellied chubby little guy standing on a boulder. The caption? "Hello, Handsome!" It's a great reminder to look deeper, beneath the obvious appearances on the surface. Many times, political animals know how to look good. They're often quite astute at putting on a good show of performance. Other employees refer to these types as empty suits. As a leader, our job is to look deeper, beneath the surface, to find those who are doing good and not just looking the part. Leaders need to be mindful that empty suits don't deliver the goods.

Number 9: Authority claimed is authority gained. I believe that we needn't worry about whether we have the authority to act or how much actual authority we have. Instead, we need to focus on doing the right thing. As Nike says, "Just Do It!" When confronted with one of those moments of truth, employees need to act decisively and not wait to be told what to do. Now with action comes accountability, so I must be clear on this. When you act, you're accountable for your actions. But acting and being decisive is infinitely better than being paralyzed by indecision. That's not leadership. That's cowardice.

Number 10: I'm self-employed. I'm an entrepreneur in the performance leasing business. This final credo may seem a little silly. But it's been very liberating to me through the years as I was coming up through the ranks in the corporate world. My father always used to say to me, "The only job security you have is your head and your hands." We should never count on a company to provide job security. Only *you* can provide job security by your work ethic, intellect, and passion to make a difference. This credo underpins my courage to take action in any moment of decision and not to wait for management to tell me what to do. It can be a little risky. Remember, there's that accountability thing lurking behind every decision you make. But for me, this has been a liberating and important mental philosophy in my work life. It has helped me to speak with conviction what I truly feel versus spouting business rhetoric, often termed euphemistically as the *party line*. At the end of the day, I believe a company hires people to be themselves. You weren't hired to be a clone of anyone else. To me, this is the true call to leadership action, to make your mark uniquely and individually in your organization, your family, and the world. Put your thumbprints wherever you are. And make your business a better place for your having been there.

In summary, when it comes to self-awareness, I simply encourage each person to develop his or her own list of credos. It can be considered your own roadmap for leadership. At the end of the day, Somerset Maugham is right. No one knows the three rules for creating great leaders. Leadership is not a common set of rules. Leadership must be from the heart, not the head, and each of us has a different approach. But if you use your personal credos to help you set the vision, set the example, and create a sense of community among your team, your family, your hometown, you will truly begin to fully realize your potential as a high-impact leader.

My Soft-Side Philosophical Nugget: *Why is the soft side so hard with regards to authenticity? We make it harder than it has to be when we do not take the time for intense personal reflection to know our personal values or our leadership credos. Leadership is a journey. It begins with self-awareness. It is rooted in the authenticity of your values. These, author Bill George suggests, are derived from those crucible events in our lives, and everyone's story is unique. But when you lead with heart, centered on the core values you hold dear, you will not only give the gift of authenticity to yourself, but you'll be a leader that others will follow. And their energies will be willingly directed at helping you achieve your vision for a better place. Their results will amaze you. That is the true impact of authentic leadership and the secret sauce for leaders in the twenty-first century.*

Chapter 8: Big Yellow Taxi

They paved paradise
And put up a parking lot
With a pink hotel, a boutique
And a swinging hot spot
Don't it always seem to go
That you don't know what you've got
'Til it's gone
They paved paradise
And put up a parking lot
Words and Music by Joni Mitchell (1970)

It's amazing so many interpretations are ascribed to the title of this instantly recognizable song of the '70s. That "big yellow taxi" has been interpreted as everything from a Canadian police wagon that is taking away a wayward father to jail to a literal yellow taxi delivering a death notice during the Vietnam War. In her own words, Joni Mitchell says:

> *I wrote "Big Yellow Taxi" on my first trip to Hawaii. I took a taxi to the hotel, and when I woke up the next morning, I threw back the curtains and saw these beautiful green mountains in*

> *the distance. Then, I looked down and there was a parking lot as far as the eye could see, and it broke my heart … this blight on paradise. That's when I sat down and wrote the song.*

Makes sense to me. The song captures almost whimsically the inevitable change that occurs in the name of progress. And the mere fact that so many interpretations exist as to its meaning makes this anthem the perfect metaphor for how change is so variably perceived by human beings in the business organization. We all interpret it through our own filters.

While I agree with whoever said, "When change stops, life stops," I've always believed that the only human being that really likes change is a wet baby. Most of us resist it, even while claiming to be open-minded to it. The reality is that change can be (and usually is) hard. Yet it seems today that businesses are continually transitioning and being tossed about by the winds of external change, internal change, and typically both.

Managers and leaders are the purveyors of this steady diet of change to the employees of the organization. Many times managers offer their own spin to emphasize the positives of the change and its impact on their teams. Sometimes this spinning can become a daunting task, given most people's inherent resistance and skepticism coupled with the fact that many changes do have perceived or genuine negative impact on people, especially in this era of cost cutting and benefits changes. Most of us aren't wet babies, however. We're pretty content babies, actually, and we're not clamoring for more change. We actually want stability and security. That security is usually assigned to the devil we know versus the devil we don't. Change is a threat. And though our world might not be a paradise when viewed from a hotel window, we don't want it paved over either. Thus, in periods of intense transitional change, what's a leader to do?

I may break ranks with traditional thought here, because I don't think a leader merely puts a positive spin on implemented changes designed or imposed as edicts from higher-ups. I think a leader has an important role in change, but if the change stinks, I don't believe people find it credible for a leader to attempt to dress it up as something that it isn't. Again, authenticity is the rule in this circumstance.

Philosophy @ Work

I led a business unit that strived to maintain a healthy work-life balance commitment. As a result, we subsidized employee participation in local health clubs. I viewed it as a values commitment. If we said we're committed to work-life balance, we had to walk the talk. At the time, of the thirty divisions in the company, ours was one of only five that offered this support. It wasn't widely subscribed to within any of the divisions, but for the 30 to 35 percent of employees who participated in health club fitness programs, it was a treasured benefit.

Unfortunately, the vice president of human services and my peer made a unilateral decision to force all divisions offering this benefit to discontinue it. In my view, there was some logic to it, as it was a benefit not all employees received. But on the other hand, all employees could have utilized it but for their own personal reasons elected not to. I was not pleased by the unilateral decision, issued without dialogue, so I enlisted the help of my other division peers who likewise offered the benefit and put together an aggressive campaign to maintain the benefit at the discretion of the divisional leader. I lost the battle, but not without significant resistance, including taking my concerns all the way to the CEO's

office. I'm sure I spent considerable political capital, but the principle was worth fighting for. I never advertised my fight to my employees, but somehow, through the grapevine, they knew.

I announced the imposed change, and I made no excuses or attempted any positive spin for the company's rationale. I simply explained that we would implement the change as directed. Though I did not agree with it, I asked them to support the corporate decision without dispute. I assured them that it had been thoroughly discussed, and while disappointing, it was now my role to support the overall decision, and I did. I likewise expected their support.

No one was terribly happy, but they complied without grousing. I allowed a rigorous discussion and what some might call venting. The decision was unpopular, and I could not fake it. I knew in my heart that I could not "spin it" and authentically spoke my truth. At the end of the day, that was a principle I could not compromise.

But beyond courageously and authentically challenging imposed changes, there is another role for leaders in the realm of change. Indeed, I believe that a true leader must likewise *instigate* change, change that is spawned by his vision or her realization of what is versus what should be or what can be. That's the type of change I'd like to speak to. Not the kind that is imposed, but the kind that is created by a leader who essentially reaches out to her team and says, "Take my hand; follow me."

As a leader, one must accept the responsibility to cause change that inspires others to follow. Leaders set a new course or take new directions to reach a goal. Sometimes a leader must say, "Let me make this perfectly clear. We do *not* intend to do business as usual, nor should we." As management guru Tom Peters espouses, companies have trouble creating the change they need due to inertia. Managers are wary of making mistakes, and understandably so. After all, managers don't get paid for screwing things up. But Tom Peters notes that innovation requires "organized forgetting." In his words, it requires strategic forgetfulness. To operate successfully in the age of the Internet, social networking sites, and globalization, businesses must forget some of the limiting paradigms generally accepted as givens in their current environment.

I've also heard Peters go on to say, "Management administrates the status quo, and most good work is done in defiance of management. The essence of all success is screwing things up." In other words, success proceeds from changing things. In fact, if people never did outrageous things, they'd never make any progress. I submit that if you had no failures this past year, it could mean that you didn't lead very much. I'm not saying you weren't busy. I'm not saying you didn't work hard and do good work. I'm confident that you did. But leaders don't stop there. The future won't allow managers to comfortably manage the status quo. Progress comes through change, so the questions you should be continually asking yourself are very simply these: What did I do differently? What *could* I have done? What improvements and changes did I *lead*? What changes *must* I lead?

Leaders dare to be different. They dare to change the way business is being done. Leaders pursue innovation. They possess and exhibit the courage to try new ideas and yes, have the confidence to risk failure. This really isn't a new concept. In fact, to pilfer shamelessly from a popular insurance company's slogan, it's so easy a caveman did it. Here's a prehistoric visual that illustrates the point. This is a very simplified representation of an actual petroglyph discovered in a cave in Southern France. It comes from my friend Dr. Aaron Buchko, Professor of Management for Bradley University's Foster College of Business.

Prehistoric Cave Drawing

Paleontologists examined this drawing to determine what it conveyed. They concluded that it represented but one word. That one word is *leadership*! The only character in this drawing with eyes is the leader. This depicts vision, and as we've discussed, vision is indeed a key element of effective leadership. Interestingly, the leader is also drawn larger than the rest of the stick figures. While I don't believe that his larger size is intended to depict positional power, hierarchy, or chain of command, I do think that it says something about the importance or significance of leadership. I think the leader is drawn larger to depict the importance of leadership to *growth and survival!*

Perhaps his was a lone voice spoken courageously but contrary to the general perspective of the tribe. These other hunters would simply do the same things they've always done before. One might say, "Hey, we've never gone that way before! We don't know what's out there. We might fail!" And perhaps the next one is saying, "We've always been successful this way! Why change now?" Still, the third hunter might say, "Why don't we commission a 6 Sigma project to analyze the opportunities and assess the risks?"

But in defiance of the status quo, the larger character, the leader, is pointing to a new way, establishing a new vision, daring to take risks—and, importantly, tapping into their hearts with the promise of greater opportunity, greater potential that translates into a greater chance for survival. Indeed, I agree with the scientists' conclusion that the perfect interpretation for the cave drawing is leadership. It's doing things differently than past methods. It is honoring the past, yes, but it does not accept the traditional methods that have brought prior success as the only right methods for tomorrow. Leaders must focus their attention on the one element of their businesses that can make a difference in the future, the one element they must continually nurture and grow. And that element is people.

Leadership also requires courage and planning. I'm sure you've heard the old adage "If you do what you've always done, you'll continue to get what you've always got!" Leaders are not timid. They dare to think big and dare to risk escaping the proverbial box. You can't be a leader until you act like one. And you can't act like one until you're willing to learn to be one by stepping outside of the bounds of comfortable management methodologies.

I find the following story fascinating. It is widely reported that Fred Smith, who founded Federal Express, wrote his master's thesis on a radical new way to do express delivery. Yet his professor gave him a grade of "C" with this reported comment: "The concept is interesting and well-formed, but in order to earn better than a C, the idea must be feasible." In other words, "Yours was a well-written dissertation, Fred, but it can't be done." Why did the professor rain on Smith's brilliant idea? The idea was so radical and so *completely* innovative that the professor was unable to see how it could be accomplished. But as we now know, Smith's idea created an entirely new industry! It took courage and planning, and it took a bold new vision.

There are some caveats about planning worth mentioning, however. While planning is important, action eats planning for lunch. Consider this anecdote regarding General Douglas MacArthur. During World War II, MacArthur called an army engineer and asked, "How long will it take to build a bridge across this river?" The engineer said it would take three days, and MacArthur replied, "Good, start drawing up the plans." Three days later MacArthur decided to see how the bridge project was going. He called the engineer and asked when it would be ready. The engineer said, "Immediately, General. You can send the troops across it today. Unless, of course, you want to wait until the plans are done; then it will take a little longer!"

Leaders embrace risk taking. Consider another example. By 1486, King Ferdinand and Queen Isabella had studied the new world voyage plans that Columbus laid out for over four years. Finally, although fearing it was crazy, they funded it. Columbus went on his mission, and it generated a 50,000 percent return on investment! Indeed, leaders cannot afford to get locked into the false security of the status quo.

I'm reminded of a caption from an old Calvin & Hobbes cartoon. Calvin says, "You know you can step into the road tomorrow and get run over by a cement truck. That's why my motto is live for the moment. What's yours?"

Hobbes, pondering a moment, finally says, "Look down the road." In other words, keep focusing on the future. Keep moving. Keep evolving. As author David Siegel says, companies today must "futurize their enterprise." It's clear that today's competitive world is changing constantly, and businesses will need to adapt to survive. Changing market conditions, new technologies, and more globally cost-competitive companies will emerge.

Frankly, the pace of change in today's world is staggering. Author Jim Collins has stated, "In a world of constant change, the fundamentals are more important than ever." He goes on to explain that the "what" of businesses today—things like strategy, tactics, and technology—is changing so rapidly, that companies rarely get it right as they noodle through future impacts and their tactics to address them. Collins suggests that it is more important to focus on the "who" of business rather than the "what." In other words, we must focus on the people side of enterprise. It is people who execute the *what*, rendering them infinitely more important than strategy!

Again, the responsible thing for leaders to do is not merely to react to change but to *drive* it. Leaders must be the proactive catalysts that shape the future of their business rather than sit back in fear as the victim of the inevitable changes that face us.

One more thing is critical in tackling the uncertainties of the future. Besides adaptability, a leader must understand the importance of listening. The interpretation of the Chinese character for listening tells us something about the significance of that critical leadership skill. Listening clearly involves the ears, but the symbol used in the Chinese language also encompasses the eyes, the whole being, and importantly, the *heart*. Years ago, I heard an after-dinner speaker, General Perry Smith, speak to the importance of listening to people and advised the practice of "squinting with your ears." Let me give you an example that shows the results possible by listening with the heart. You might say this example shows the power of "taking it to heart," and that's a perfect descriptor. Let me hearken back to Federal Express.

Philosophy @ Work

The vision at Federal Express is simple: "Every package shipped every night!" One of my favorite stories is about a FedEx employee who, near the end of his shift, noticed a package that had not been shipped. It happened to be a human organ, desperately needed for a surgery the next morning. This shipping dock employee, on his own, chartered a plane and personally took the package to its destination. It cost $4,800 to get that organ there. This person was named employee of the year. Because their vision is "every package shipped every night," he did exactly what he should have done. He took a risk perhaps, but in his heart, it wasn't risky. He simply made it happen, no matter the cost. The employee heard the company vision, and he listened with his heart. He took it to heart.

And you can be confident that the leadership of Federal Express spoke volumes by naming this employee its employee of the year. His story is a compelling testimony to commitment and the power of listening with heart, and it reveals the undeniable importance of leadership's impact on company culture.

My Soft-Side Philosophical Nugget: *Why is the soft side so hard when it comes to leading change? We make it harder than it has to be when we too often shrink from authenticity and fail to challenge detrimental changes. And we too often fail to touch people's hearts by communicating a clear vision of a better future. We make the mistake that spinning imposed change is leading change. Instigating change follows from creating a vision. And it involves courageous risk taking. When leaders dare to be different, when they communicate a compelling vision for change that inspires people's emotional commitment, and when they let go of the status quo and shed traditional paradigms, they affect the culture and employees in a way that unleashes them to reach* *beyond their comfort zones and to perform with passion, innovation, and extraordinary commitment. They flag down that "big yellow taxi" and hop on board. Collins says, "Put the right people on the bus." When I think of leading transformational change, my ride is a big yellow taxi, headed for a promised land called the future.*

Chapter 9: When You Say Nothing At All

It's amazing how you can speak right to my heart
Without saying a word you can light up the dark
Try as I may I could never explain
What I hear when you don't say a thing
The smile on your face lets me know that you need me
There's a truth in your eyes sayin' you'll never leave me
The touch of your hand says you'll catch me if ever I fall
You say it best when you say nothing at all
Words and Music by Paul Overstreet and Don Schlitz (1988)

Nobel winner Albert Schweitzer once said, "Example is not the main thing in influencing others. It is the only thing." Obviously, my father never won the Nobel Peace Prize, but he had his own unique and effective way of emphasizing the importance of being a good example. He used to rib me if I made a harmless mistake with this admonition: "Don't worry, Billy, everybody's good for something, even if it's being a bad example!"

My dad enjoyed teasing me. He loved to laugh, and nothing made him smile more than an oft-repeated exchange that occurred regularly between us as he returned from work. He'd greet me with a grin and ask, "Were you good today, Billy?"

"Yes, Dad," I'd say, knowing what was coming.

"Did you get paid for being good?" he'd ask.

"Nope," I would readily admit.

"Then you're good for nothing!" he'd exclaim, laughing as if this were always a fresh new gag. But it wasn't new. He'd do that sometimes several times a week, and always with the same reaction—a robust belly laugh. Often he'd add, "But were you a good example today, right bud?"

As silly as this was, it drove his point home. Doing good—doing the right thing—was not a task to be performed for hire. It was an obligation without expectation of compensation. To him it was, in short, a duty. One he modeled for me, one he expected me to follow, and one he'd delight in when I said I'd been good for nothing. I can still hear his laughter, and I'm grateful that he taught me that there is no traffic jam in the extra mile. Traveling that extra mile to do good is our calling. He didn't preach it. He modeled it. He was my quiet example.

Today, not only in the business world but also in the world at large, there is no shortage of bad examples. Business, being composed of human beings, is merely a subset or microcosm of our general society. So it is filled with examples of the all-too-human frailty we possess. We learn of a new disclosure every day as the media has an unending source of new material to report some notable individual's fall from grace, including respected people, celebrated people—be they sports figures, entertainers, political leaders, or religious and business leaders. All are merely flawed human beings who provide continual fodder for the common lamentation that there are simply precious few positive role models today. Our celebrity-obsessed culture is hungry for them, but we wrongly assign role model status and expectations to mere celebrity rather than to character.

Mark Twain's quote rings true, "Few things are harder to put up with than the annoyance of a good example." But sadly today, we are not sufficiently annoyed. Nonetheless, leaders are called to set a good example, and doing so speaks volumes even without words. Failing to set a positive example sells newspapers with more words than most offenders would like.

What differentiates exemplary leaders? In my view, it is their steadfast willingness to do good (regardless the consequences) over merely looking good. And that comes from commitment, a deep commitment that avoids the seduction of the typical trappings of power or influence. And it is a powerful example for others who are most definitely watching. This maxim, attributed to St. Francis of Assisi, applies: "Preach the Gospel. And if necessary, use words."

Why do leaders lose their way? Like Narcissus, they fall in love with their own reflection. They begin to believe that they are, in fact, so "pretty." And this problem can be exacerbated when the leader's support network or the team that surrounds him is selected to ensure that those praises continue to be sung. I've mentioned previously, however, that when people stop telling you the truth, they're of marginal value. A leader must strive to set the example to embrace truth, even painful truths. When employees begin to tell you what you want to hear, instead of the truth you need to hear, look at yourself. The environment that makes them believe it's safer to spin truth rather than to be honest with the boss is a web of *your* construction. The best example you can provide is one of commitment to truth, integrity, and honest communications. Mark Twain also remarked, "When someone else blows your horn, the music is twice as sweet!" But when they only toot *to* you instead of complimenting you to others, it can signal a dangerous brand of flattery.

I've often reflected on my own example. Clearly I have disappointed others and myself at times. But I keep trying. Persistence is more important than perfection. Recently, this was driven home by an experience with my oldest son, Michael. In 2008, we cofounded a leadership development company named Fullsail Leadership. It was not my idea, not in the least. I was enjoying board work, public speaking, teaching, and consulting. I had no intention of becoming an entrepreneur. Yet Mike persisted. He was so committed to spreading what he deemed to be an important leadership message and philosophy of service to younger employees that he doggedly and determinedly convinced me that this message needed to be heard. He had a vision to create a leadership development company founded with a mission to touch people's hearts, provoke their minds, and liberate their voices as authentic leaders. To be honest, it humbled me. I was not even aware that Mike had paid much attention to my espoused leadership philosophy through the years. In fact, I frankly thought he was a bit weary of hearing it.

I remember one day when he was just a teenager. I presume he had grown tired of my continual use of leadership quotations when at one moment he quipped, "Dad, why do you always quote dead people? Don't you know that shows an absence of original thought?" Through my chuckling, I told him there was wisdom in the ages and offered no apology for tapping into it. Apparently, he was listening more than I realized.

Philosophy @ Work

We started our company, and during our initial public seminar, Mike was asked the following question by an attendee: "How has your father's leadership philosophy affected you and your own leadership approach? " Mike paused for a moment and then began to respond. What he said touched me and caused me to reflect upon my own father's quiet example and impact upon my life. Here's what he said:

Thanks for that great question. It's actually been on my mind for some time. I can honestly say that Bill's philosophy cannot and will not be my own ... He wouldn't want this and didn't raise me this way. I believe in tipping your hat to those who have preceded you, and I certainly do tip my hat to my father. After all, it was his philosophy that I believed in so deeply to cofound Fullsail Leadership. But to directly answer the question, Bill's philosophy has taught me that it is okay to make mistakes. Leaders are human. But I must have confidence in my abilities, virtues, my values, and myself as a person. Yet also recognize that I am flawed and will make mistakes. At the end of the day, Bill taught me to have a loving tolerance of who I am as well as a loving tolerance of who (and what) I am not. This way of thinking, this philosophy on leadership, has allowed me an opportunity to reflect on myself so that I may deny ego/self in my attempt to serve others, the organization, customers, colleagues, my team, and my family and also realize that I have to persistently "sail on." The journey continues each unfolding mile.

I was stunned. I had never really sat down and spoken those things to Mike. And I actually had said nothing at all about him developing a personal leadership philosophy. I was just authentically myself, and he did the rest. What impressed me so much about Mike's answer was his catching on to the theme of courage—the courage to try things, knowing he'll make mistakes, but consistently sailing on.

Over many years, I have observed far too much tentativeness in young people coming into the business world, and I think there are a number of reasons for it. One of the reasons is something I call parental hovering. I fear that parents are crippling young people today by this practice. Here's what I mean. From the earliest days of childhood, parents tote kids to T-ball, traveling soccer, dance lessons, gymnastics, Indian Guides, Indian Princesses, modeling, and 4-H. When I was a kid, we played baseball on a dirt lot with cardboard bases, tattered baseballs, and cracked baseball bats wound with electrical tape. Today, it seems that suburban kids can't play ball without uniforms, on perfectly manicured fields with a fence and even sometimes with lights!

Then comes high school. Parents go *with* their kids to homecoming and prom to presumably chaperone and often invasively go to the designated rendezvous spot to take photos for the momentous occasion. This didn't happen when I was a kid, and thank God! Then comes college. It seems that all college students have cell phones, and statistics say that they are continually texting and talking with their parents over five to ten times per week! I'm all for staying connected, but I fear that such hovering creates an extended state of what Admiral Hyman Rickover, father of the modern nuclear navy, termed "suspended adolescence."

This is akin to 24/7 tethering, an extension of the umbilical cord, in my view, and I think it keeps young people in an overly cautious and dependent frame of mind. It actually limits their courage and stunts their decision-making experiences. Is it so unusual then to see young people entering the workplace likewise looking for that continual shepherding, that tether, that safety net? I saw it all the time, and I think it contributes to a crippling of young people's independence. They exhibit no shortage of ambition, but they exhibit an unwillingness to step out, risk mistakes, or reach for extraordinary goals. In short, they want to play it safe, but they want to be the CEO in five years time! That simply doesn't compute.

Today, in the business world, young people enter the playground with the other big kids, and their parents are not there. So they latch onto any form of safety. And all too often, that's the safety of a manager who controls and presumably protects them from venturing out into the risky world of making decisions. They tell them what to do. How to do it. When to do it. What not to do. It's a managerial form of hovering. And it cripples young employees. Leaders must let go. Let these young employees learn and make choices—make their own decisions—attempt to make their own unique contributions. Managerial hovering is limiting their growth by enabling continual insulation from the hard, cold realities of personal accountability, limiting their opportunities to learn from mistakes, and excluding them from the risky opportunities to make their unique mark, possibly achieving extraordinary results.

It's no surprise that I see so much tentativeness. I see young people all too willing to wait for management before risking their own initiative. Certainly they have fears about their authority level, fears about making mistakes, and fears about getting into trouble or getting a strike against them or their career. They seek that safety net eagerly, so when management gives guidance in the form of some formalized process map or strict limits that will presumably safely guide them rather than forcing self-reliance, it's gobbled up with thanks. Of course, a business culture that overemphasizes management control in lieu of leadership breeds this in spades. It does a disservice to these talented people hired into the firm.

Instead of perpetuating the tethering, managers need to let go. Let new people experiment, swim on their own in the pool with the sharks. Of course, some might consider this old school, a form of sink or swim. Perhaps some regard this as a callous leadership approach. I disagree. I consider it a gift that engenders independence, learning, and risk taking.

Consider the controversial practice of teaching babies to swim before they can walk. It's the only activity where babies are completely independent, especially before they can walk or crawl unaided. They are placed in the swimming pool in deep water, under the watchful eye of a caring parent. The water supports their weight, and they are free to move their legs and arms as much as they want. Proponents suggest that babies actually love it!

Of course parents and managers must be mindful and guided by the mantra of "Do no harm." And it goes without saying that this must be approached in a spirit of "Teach me; don't hurt me." There is no benefit in traumatizing a child to learn a new skill, nor is there any benefit in traumatizing an employee in a new position. Being in tune with feelings and perceptions of those we are leading is important, because the immediate and long-term consequences of indifference can be significant both emotionally and mentally for the long term. But when supported and guided with sensitivity, people—even babies—can perform extraordinarily well and beyond what you might intuitively believe are the limits of their capability or experience.

But you might ask, is a baby swimming underwater safe? Consider this. When a baby goes underwater, something called their "diving reflex" kicks in. The same sort of thing happens when you swallow. The epiglottis closes over and blocks the throat so no water can get through. That's why babies often swim underwater with their mouths open! This reflex lasts up until eighteen months of age or so. After that point, we must teach toddlers and older children how to swim in a different way.

As teachers and leaders in business, the intent must be focused on sowing seeds of understanding with kindness. This will bear fruit of a most wondrous kind—independent, self-reliant, caring human beings, *and* very effective decision makers for the company. When cultivated by a foundation of understanding, kindness, and patience (never rushing), infant/toddler swimming provides a unique opportunity to unlock the child's potential and growth on many levels. Liberated young employees will experience this same growth when encouraged to "swim" on their own, and the business will thrive when we allow them into the pool of learning by experience and experiment.

That's the leadership philosophy implied when I say sink or swim. It is not to be indifferent or callous. It is to support them at all times while not encumbering or limiting them with too much handholding. Leaders should create an environment for young employees to learn to swim … to be independent … to grow. But the leader, unlike the micro-manager, can't do the strokes for them. I tell young people to trust their instincts. They won't drown, and a caring leader gets in the pool with them. That's the key. It is not abandonment; it is buoyant support that permits their independence.

Philosophy @ Work

As a young field representative on my first assignment in California, I was just beginning to learn the business. I was the service representative supporting a number of large Caterpillar dealers. Any customer contact I had was always in the company of the dealer, at their insistence. This was probably wise, because I was new and was just learning the ropes. What I didn't realize was that dealers became very selective about which customers they'd allow me to see. In other words, I was being insulated in some ways from the full measure of truth about customer perceptions and satisfaction with either the dealers or with Caterpillar products. That was soon to change.

After about three months on the job, I was asked to host a visiting European manager, Mr. Francis Cuttat, who was interested in learning more about Cat's North American business. Because my territory was the second largest market in the United States, this gent was assigned to me for a week of travel. I dutifully put together a round robin of dealer visits and, on the appointed day, picked up Francis at the airport. After some initial cordial chitchat, he promptly asked me, "So what customers are we going to be visiting?" I fumbled awkwardly but finally admitted that we would be visiting no customers, only dealers. He looked at me with surprise and said somewhat sternly, "I already know dealers, Bill. I want to know US customers. Your job is to support customers first! Never forget that!" I said that I was told by the dealer never to visit a customer without them, and he retorted, "That's precisely why you must!"

Well, after some hasty reworking of the week's agenda, we ended up visiting over twenty customers—some with the dealer participating, but surprisingly, some without. I often look back at that experience in my early career and marvel at how his simple insistence that I get in front of customers rather than merely dealers literally changed my entire perception of my role. I learned that I was Caterpillar to these customers. I learned that the dealer provides an invaluable role supporting purchasers of our products, but that we factory types should never insulate ourselves from the end user; that customers provide invaluable and unvarnished truth about our performance and the performance of our dealers.

I learned so much that week. And it altered the course of my focus from that point forward. I became, with Francis's encouragement, not merely a dealer representative, but a passionate customer advocate. I was swimming on my own, and it changed my life. Oftentimes, I found myself actually leading my dealer people to engage more proactively in meeting customers and getting to know them even better than before.

Of course young people today are ambitious, and that's a good thing. However, this can also contribute to tentativeness, as they are anxious that everyone is watching them. The truth is, everyone *is*! But this is a great opportunity, not something to be feared. When young employees come on board, leaders must nurture their independence but also honestly explain that they are, in fact, in a fish bowl. They can swim to all corners of their environment. And it should be encouraged. They should be permitted to explore the far reaches of their environment to make their mark. As leadership is about grooming the next generation of leaders, our role is to liberate them to make the right choices and to explore the right places with an aim to make something happen to change that environment for the better.

My Soft-Side Philosophical Nugget: *Why is the soft side so hard when it comes to setting an example? We make it harder than it has* *to be when we tell rather than show. Managers are telling too much and not showing enough. We say it best not with our talk but with our walk as we model exemplary behaviors. The old adage applies: "Your walk talks and your talk talks, but your walk talks louder than your talk talks." Leaders must simply walk their talk. And they say it best when they say nothing at all. Leaders must encourage young employees to believe that they weren't hired to administer the status quo or to play it safe. They were hired to lead, to grow into leadership impact and to make a difference. Sure, that may feel a bit overwhelming because it puts them in the uncomfortable position of making choices, of swimming when they'd rather be tethered to a float. Their choices have consequences and therefore don't feel safe. But instead of a manager who tells employees what to do, be a leader who explains the criteria expected for how to make choices. Get in the pool with them, but let 'em swim!*

Chapter 10: Fame

You ain't seen the best of me yet
Give me time I'll make you forget the rest
I got more in me
And you can set it free
I can catch the moon in my hands
Don't you know who I am
Remember my name
Fame
I'm gonna live forever
I'm gonna learn how to fly
High
I feel it coming together
People will see me and cry
Fame
I'm gonna make it to heaven
Light up the sky like a flame
Fame
I'm gonna live forever
Baby remember my name
Remember
Remember

Remember
Remember
Remember
Remember
Remember
Remember

Words and Music by Michael Gore and Dean Pitchford (1980)

I've always said that each of us is actually three people: who we are, who we think we are, and who we want others to think we are. That's why self-awareness, which is a lifelong pursuit, is so essential to authentic leadership. I tend to view life as a journey that strives to bring these three disparate perspectives into harmony—into wholeness—such that the three are actually one and the same. To me, that harmonization would ensure a healthy self-awareness and healthy state of being.

Climbing the corporate ladder sometimes puts these three internal perceptions in conflict. It can be a challenge to fit comfortably in the new "skin' of an executive level leadership position. Indeed, there are some trappings with each successive rung of the ladder. Sometimes it can create a cognitive dissonance and contradiction within the leader that is perceived by employees as a lack of authenticity—as if something about the rarified air of executive leadership somehow changes the person—and they are perceived as having become aloof, detached, or arrogant. It might not be fair or accurate, but these perceptions exist, especially when a competitive peer is promoted above his colleagues.

Indeed, there have many been times in my career when associates have been frustrated by executive leadership and have lamented that "something happens to people when they reach the executive ranks." They wrongly assume that it is the position or rank that creates the problem, when in fact it is more likely the conflicted self-perceptions within the leader that are projected externally. One friend noted, "These guys forgot what it's like to be in the lower ranks. They apparently think you merely speak things into existence. And the trouble is, they never remember ever making a bad play."

I've seen this as well. Managers who have been "bumped" upstairs often seem to change. Perhaps it's insulation. Perhaps it comes with the trappings of hierarchical power where organizations tend to deify the top dogs. Perhaps it's actually a sense of personal vulnerability and fear, meaning that these anointed ones look around and question, "Why me?"

In those positions, it's tempting to build artificial walls that ensure that no one will discover that nagging fear lurking inside—that these managers are just as unsure and afraid of making mistakes in this bigger fish bowl as those below them. They recognize that there is a lot of talent in the organization, and they feel blessed and fortunate, of course, to have "made it," but within them that still small voice sounds notes of personal doubt, fear, and anxiety. "Do I really deserve to be here? What if I'm found out to be less than the requirements of the position?" It can be scary.

As an elected officer and vice president of Caterpillar, Inc., I committed to coming into the officer's position as "Bill," and leaving the position as "Bill." In reality, I feel grateful that many of the great employees I was privileged to serve actually made me a "better Bill." But it does seem there are two approaches among executives in response to hierarchical achievement. One approach involves humility and a steadfast commitment to remain true to who they really are. Another approach is at best supreme confidence, and at worst outright arrogance. These are those executives who indeed enjoy the fame and, over time, forget that they've ever made a bad play. Of course, I have a philosophical perspective about it all.

Philosophy @ Work

I was once considering leaving my company after about five years to take a position with another firm. I told my boss, thinking he'd wail and gnash his teeth and plead with me to stay. Instead, he simply said, "Okay. If you leave, there will be ten people in line to take your place." Though I was admittedly a bit personally crushed, it was a valuable lesson for me. I recalled that old adage that merits remembrance: "When you leave, it's like pulling your hand from a bucket filled with water. No hole." But that's not what I wanted my impact to be. I decided right then that when I did eventually leave, my thumbprints had better be there. I was not going to merely occupy time and space. I committed to ensure that there would be forensic evidence of my having been there. Not for my own fame, but evidence that would long outlast my tenure in the company. I began to think of legacy and building the next generation of leaders. But I wasn't certain how to go about it.

About five years later, an insightful leader named George provided the answer, and I owe a great deal to him. George came in new as the leader of a division I was assigned to. He was the new "big boss." I had been at the company about ten years at this point, and was a supervisor reporting to George. Shortly after his arrival, he called each direct report into his office individually for what I basically thought was to be an obligatory get-acquainted session and conversation about goals, objectives, and challenges for the business.

One of the first questions George asked me was "What is your life plan?" I wasn't listening well, I suppose, because I started fumbling with some lame answer about my career plan. Problem was, I didn't have a career plan. I told George that I did not define myself by a rung on a ladder; I was merely committed to keep my head down and perform to the best of my ability, blah, blah, blah. I told him I wanted to build a legacy of service, and I told him if I got promoted, fine. If I didn't, that was fine too, as long as I was making a valuable contribution.

The truth is, I had neither a career plan nor a life plan. But this leader listened patiently and when I finished my awkward response said, "I didn't ask you what your career plan was. I asked you what your life plan was." From this subtle distinction, we discussed things that were important to me—values, personal life, passions, interests, and life goals. George encouraged me to write down my values. He encouraged me to write down my life goals.

With George's support and mentoring, I undertook his challenge. It was so timely at this critical point in my career as a new supervisor. Over the course of a few weeks, I developed and wrote my personal credos. I began to understand exactly what I stood for and what principles and values would guide me as a leader. And from George's example, as a leader who cared, I learned the importance of a leader's legacy and the power and impact a leader can have upon a human heart. I tried to quit worrying about positional achievement. I became more concerned about impact.

The paradox is that as I focused more on legacy, the results came and were noticed, and I was successively promoted almost to my surprise. Fame for me was not about my achievement or personal position. If people were to remember my leadership, it would have to come in the form of a legacy of leaders who came after me. George gave me the permission to create the leadership roadmap I was searching for. Indeed, I owe George a lot.

So the question is, as someone who believes strongly in the concept of legacy, how does one leave indelible thumbprints on the company and upon the people we're privileged to lead? Henry

Ford once said, "You can't build a reputation on what you're going to do." So clearly it's not about occupying a lofty position alone, about pulling strings and issuing orders. It's about action. What did you actually do? And for me, it's less about great programs conceived or implemented; it's less about the outstanding results gained; it's less about the impact you've had upon the stock price.

Fundamentally, if you accept that leadership is truly about building the next generation of leaders, your only genuine concern for legacy should be your personal impact and the development of those who come after you, those you've led, empowered, developed, and nurtured to be leaders in their own right. These people, the future leaders, will be your living legacy. Perhaps this will not always attributed to you, but that's not important. It's not about Super Bowl rings and MVP trophies. Leadership is about serving and touching people's hearts. And that will not rust or corrode over time. It lasts well beyond you, and as your legacy is paid forward, it outlasts the momentary fame of a positional box in the executive hierarchy. That will merely become but a footnote in company history. The real play is the impact upon human beings. And that brings me to the importance of a leader's role in mentoring.

Anais Nin wrote, "There came a time when the pressure to remain tight in a bud was overcome by the pressure to bloom." Each of our employees can bloom. As leaders, that is your calling, to facilitate that blooming. But what do you know about the word mentor? The word actually comes from Greek mythology. Mentor was an old friend of Odysseus. Odysseus entrusted his household and his son to Mentor when he joined the coalition that sailed against Troy. Mentor became the guide of Odysseus' son, Telemachus, giving him safe and prudent counsel. Wise and trusted advisers have been called mentors since then. I find it fascinating that the original mentor was actually a substitute father figure.

Not long ago, I spoke with a young African American woman who had recently joined the company. She spoke of her daunting challenge to tackle the corporate world with little or no guidance, and she spoke of the importance of reaching out and talking to people, people who have held similar positions and learned valuable lessons she could learn from. Obviously, I commended her insight, but I counseled her as well that one of the keys of a successful mentoring relationship is the importance of actually being "mentor-able." I'm reminded of Emerson, who said, "Our chief want in life is to find someone who inspires us to be what we already know we can be." And I think that's an important challenge to everyone.

Younger, inexperienced employees are not empty vessels. They are *not* programmed to sit at the foot of a mentor and be filled with wisdom and the magical keys to success. If that's someone's view of being mentored or mentoring, it's a flawed view. Socrates once took a young mentoree to a lake; stuck his head into the water, and asked, "What do you want?" After a minute in the water, he pulled him up and the mentoree gasped, "Wisdom." Socrates pushed his head into the water again and after another minute asked, "What do you want?" The breathless mentoree said, "Knowledge." Socrates again pushed his head underwater and finally asked, "What do you want?" At this the mentoree gasped, "Air!" Socrates then said, "When you want wisdom and knowledge as much as you want air, you'll be ready to learn!"

Being mentor-able is as much more about an internal hunger—a commitment to grow, to serve, and to learn from the wisdom of others—than it is being an empty vessel to be filled with the knowledge of the keys to success. I counsel mentorees never to *assume*. Never assume that people know what you want when you proclaim, "I want you to mentor me." If you don't know where you're going, any road will get you there.

The qualities of being mentor-able are 1) being interested, 2) being inquisitive, with keen intellectual curiosity, 3) having initiative, 4) having an internal engine that fuels a desire to learn, 5) being ready and willing to learn about yourself—not just about the experiences and successes *or* mistakes of the mentor—and finally, 6) being mature.

But what about mentors? What makes them good teachers or advisors? An effective mentor in my mind is simply one who mentors successful students. And it's incumbent on the mentor to do three things: 1) do no harm; 2) demand and reward excellence; and 3) understand the employee's perspective. In other words, to understand both the unique individual perspective of the person mentored but also importantly to understand and embrace the unique collective identity of race, gender, or ethnicity.

Each new employee comes into the company uniquely prewired. Each has the opportunity to put his or her thumbprints on the organization—their *unique* thumbprints. I would not want to mentor someone to be a clone of me. I would simply want to unleash the full power within them. In an excellent book entitled *Wild at Heart* by John Eldredge, one of my favorite quotations is, "Let the world feel the full weight of your presence—and let 'em deal with it."

Each of us has greatness within. It may be buried deeper in some than in others, but it's there. As a mentor, we must inspire that greatness. That involves caring. The University of Illinois actually did a study on the learning ability of students. Interestingly, one of the key conclusions of all the determinants of learning ability was found to be a "teacher who cared." I encourage the philosophy of leaders as teachers in a business culture. And great teachers *care.*

It is a myth to conclude that people can pull themselves up by the bootstraps. It can't be done. You need mentors. Those who inspire.

Those who push. Those who pull. Those who help people learn from their mistakes rather than crushing them. And leaders have an obligation to be mentors. They did not achieve their positions by "pulling on their bootstraps"; so likewise, leaders should not expect that of others. Employees have an obligation to step beyond their comfort zone and to be mentor-able. They must reach out, talk to people, keep their head down, and achieve results. But employees must also find cross-functional mentors who can inspire and nurture them. It is not always about linking to a person higher up in the chain of command either. Employees must not forget that lessons can be learned from employees who aren't in positions of power or influence—and they must likewise be open to learn from any man or woman of good character, those who have stories to tell and lessons to share at every level in the organization.

And here is one final point regarding mentoring. I have a particular sensitivity for the challenges of mentoring employees of color. There is a *Harvard Business Review* article written in April 2001 entitled "Race Matters." It's written by Mr. David A. Thomas, and its subtitle is "The truth about mentoring minorities." It speaks openly about the challenges for mentoree and mentor alike. One of the important points made is that many cross-race mentoring relationships suffer from what he terms "protective hesitation"—both parties refrain from raising touchy issues. It's an important read, in my view.

In far too many companies today, the organizational chart is stuffed with predominantly white male managers. In these cultures, people of color do face unique challenges. And let's not shrink away from the intellectual honesty of that contextual reality. As leaders, we have a tremendous opportunity to tap into the strength of the diversity of our employees. Employees have a tremendous opportunity to help us achieve our goals. But it takes both—mentor and mentoree—to unleash the full power of the diversity that exists in companies. In his book, *The Wisdom of Crowds*, David Suroweicki builds a strong case for the power of diversity in problem solving. And an old Russian proverb says, "Without a shepherd, the sheep are not a flock." A shepherd provides safety, well-being, dependability, consistency, support, direction, trust, and nurturing. This is a requirement for the entire flock, not for a select few. In my mind, this is a significant challenge each leader should embrace.

My Soft-Side Philosophical Nugget:

Why is the soft side the hardest part of fame and success? We make it harder than it has to be when we lose focus on others and imagine that it is really all about us. It isn't about us. It's about them—the people we're called to develop into the future leaders for the firm. This is the legacy leaders must strive for. Not their own success or fame, but the success of those who follow. It's about leaving indelible thumbprints on the people, not on the organizational chart.

One final anecdote ... twenty-five years ago, I heard a story. A school principal and a teacher walked together into the boy's bathroom. The room had graffiti all over its stalls, walls, and halls. The teacher, in disgust, said, "We have to teach these boys how not to write on the bathroom walls." The principal reflected for a moment then replied, "They already know how not *to write on the bathroom walls. You can't teach an attitude." Well, I am advocating an attitude. You likely already intuitively know everything I've spoken of in this chapter. Now you have to exercise an attitude to make a difference. When you do commit to the legacy of building the next generation of leaders, and it is my hope and expectation that every reader of these pages do just that, you will have made your business a better place. You will have left your thumbprints. And there is no higher calling, no greater legacy, and no fame more worthy of your aspirations.*

Chapter 11: What's It All About, Alfie?

What's it all about, Alfie?
Is it just for the moment we live?
What's it all about when you sort it out, Alfie?
Are we meant to take more than we give
Or are we meant to be kind?
And if only fools are kind, Alfie,
Then I guess it's wise to be cruel.
And if life belongs only to the strong, Alfie,
What will you lend on an old golden rule?
As sure as I believe there's a heaven above, Alfie,
I know there's something much more,
Something even nonbelievers can believe in.
I believe in love, Alfie.
Without true love we just exist, Alfie.
Until you find the love you've missed you're nothing, Alfie.
When you walk let your heart lead the way
And you'll find love any day, Alfie
Words and Music by Burt Bacharach and Hal David (1967)

I love old films, and one that stands out in my memory is one I probably shouldn't have seen as a young teenager in 1966. If there were movie ratings back then, this film would have earned a double capital R. The film was called *Alfie*, and it starred Michael Caine in the title role. It was a raw look at life, and a selfish life at that, but what stands out more in my memory today is the film's title song, written by the Oscar-nominated duo of Burt Bacharach and Hal David. Indeed this movie's anthem underscores the message from Alfie's tormented life's journey: "Life's meaning and fulfillment comes from true love, not from physical pleasures or temptations, not from material gain, not from personal or business success, and not from status or fame. Purpose and fulfillment spring from love."

Purpose and passion in our working lives is not that different. As Johann Wolfgang Von Goethe said, "Not the maker of plans and promises, but rather the one who offers faithful service in small matters. This is the person who is most likely to achieve what is good and lasting."

I've shared with you before that whenever I'm asked what the function of leadership is, I always answer with three things: set the vision, set the example, and create a sense of community. When asked, "How?" I simply reply that it requires authenticity and a deep and unwavering commitment to personal values. Only then can you fulfill your destiny as a leader. That destiny is to serve. Furthermore, service is the source of true joy for the leader. In my experience, Albert Schweitzer's words ring true: "Those who have sought and found how to serve will truly be happy."

It's essential to remember that we are all called to serve not ourselves but others. Another old film favorite of mine that illustrates this beautifully is a classic holiday film starring Jimmy Stewart entitled *It's a Wonderful Life*. During the Christmas holiday season, invariably as you sit down to do some channel surfing on those cold December evenings, you'll find it in the channel guide. In my mind, it's deserving of *at least* one viewing per year, and I have made that a family tradition in my home.

George Bailey, Stewart's character, is a noble man. George grew up in mythical Bedford Falls. He is a dreamer and an adventurer at heart, scheming to trek to all parts of the world beyond the confines what he perceives to be his insignificant small-town life. But sadly, just as he's about to set off on his worldly adventures, he finds that he is trapped by the obligation of sacrifice and service to others. George's father, president of the Bailey Savings and Loan, suffers a stroke, and George must step in, albeit reluctantly, to run the family business.

George's tradition of sacrifice began at a young age. You may remember that as a small lad, George lost hearing in one ear while saving his younger brother Harry from falling through the crust of an icy pond while skating. So understandably, it's no surprise that once again, George sucks it up when duty calls. He agrees to manage the family business, and he gives up his own dreams of adventure in order to serve the people of Bedford Falls.

George ultimately marries Mary (played by the lovely Donna Reed). He soon finds himself with four kids and no exit from Bedford Falls, and circumstance by circumstance, his world crashes down upon him—including a Depression-style run on the bank caused by a careless uncle's loss of the day's receipts. Ultimately, George gives up. His life's dream is shattered. All the good he's accomplished seems for naught. In a Christmas Eve fit of anger and depression, George sets out to kill himself.

At that moment, an angel—one who hasn't yet earned his wings—named Clarence is sent to show George the error of his thinking.

George is transported to a world where it's as if he'd never been born. And he's given the gift of insight to see how people's lives would have been affected without George's service and influence. His life's work –perhaps as unintended as it was—was filled with selfless sacrifice and service to others. George eventually begins to understand.

He learns that the entire town of Bedford Falls (without him in it) would have been taken over by the mean and greedy Mr. Potter, played by Lionel Barrymore. Through this angelic, otherworldly journey, George finally realizes that his life indeed has had meaning. He may not have achieved his dream of worldly adventure, but he changed the world for so many through his dedicated service.

This film reaches to the core of the human spirit and to the goodness of service. It is rich with leadership lessons, either specifically written or implied, that underpin the answer to the Alfie's of the world and also to each one of us "What is it all about?" Indeed, here are what I consider to be some key leadership lessons from this classic film.

Number 1: Leaders come from anywhere in an organization. Anyone can be a leader. George Bailey was certainly an unlikely hero or leader. But leadership is not about position, rank, or title. The power of leadership, especially service-based leadership, comes from an ability to create trust through meaningful, committed relationships. Those come from the heart, and opening your heart to people builds relationships in which we know we can rely upon one another. Leaders don't rely on words of power. They rely on deeds of service and deeds of caring.

Number 2: Leaders act on the natural human impulse to help others. They know that self-interest doesn't make the world go round. George Bailey knew this. He sacrificed his yearning to travel. He sacrificed his education. He sacrificed his honeymoon. But in so doing, he created a much more intimate adventure with far greater impact on his world. Truly, the world would have been poorer without George Bailey's thumbprints on it. Each and every individual can play an important role in service to each other and to the greater community at large.

Number 3: Leaders recognize when courage is called for. George Bailey stood strong against the evil and conniving Mr. Potter. It no doubt was a lonely place to be, but George was acting on principle. Often, a leader will find that he or she is alone, supported only by personal principles. Authentic leaders are likewise willing to admit when they don't have the answers. They aren't afraid to ask colleagues for help. George modeled this humility in spades.

Number 4: Leaders speak truthfully. This drives an organization's culture and inspires people to stick together and have faith in one other. It is really a litmus test of organizational harmony. Anyone in a successful enterprise will tell you that having faith in one's coworkers is paramount. It's trust that leads to a healthy community.

Number 5: Leaders build community. Our lives and how we live them develop meaning, and a legacy is created not by big home runs of success but through small acts that over time make a big difference.

Number 6: Leaders encourage and enable others to realize their full potential. This is achieved by encouragement and persuasion, not by coercion or power. Just as George Bailey saved his brother's life, permitting Harry to grow and thrive and reach his potential as a decorated army air corps pilot, leaders trust the ability of others to rise to any challenge. Leaders empower others to come up with solutions that are in the best interests of the organization and the team. In other words, leaders allow others to grow and to lead. More important, they preserve and lift up the bold employee whose risk taking proved a failure.

And finally, lesson number 7: Leaders are human. They feel fear, anguish, and disappointment. They falter. They fail. They fall down. But as Clarence revealed to George, they must get back up again. Leaders do. They persevere. They overcome. George eventually decides to face the music, and in a touching final scene, those whom he so faithfully served in the past step up to serve him. It's a heartwarming moment that never fails to evoke my emotions.

Philosophy @ Work

In December of 2005, I met with 485 employees of Caterpillar's largest marketing division. I was their newly elected vice president, and I was an unknown to most of them. I knew that they were likely concerned about changes I would make. I knew that they would be worried about the "new guy" coming in with a personal agenda that would mean sweeping changes for the organization. I knew that they would want to know, and soon, which direction I would be leading them.

As the holiday season was upon us, there was a festiveness and excitement to the scene blended with this understandable angst about their new leader. I elected to hit the issue of where I would be leading them head on. I developed a presentation using Capra's It's a Wonderful Life as the theme. I began by telling them a bit of my personal background, and of course, I told them that I was honored to be appointed as the leader of this outstanding unit. I then acknowledged the elephant in the room. I told them that I was quite aware that the big question on everyone's mind was how would things be different under my leadership. Where were we headed?

What would the division look like in the future? After a long pause, I simply said, "I have no idea where I'm leading you. But I know how I am going to lead you." And with this, I presented the story of George Bailey and It's a Wonderful Life, complete with all of the leadership lessons I presented above. The feedback was astounding. I emphasized people, culture, love, service, truthfulness, humanity, and community. That was the "how" of my leadership intent. The "what" would become clearer to me as I learned about the business and its unique challenges. And I enlisted their help to teach me the business.

My approach was simple. I attempted to touch their hearts. I attempted to reach them on an emotional versus an intellectual level. And it worked. I heard universal positive feedback. It was clear to them that whatever changes I would initiate would be rooted in the principles and values of my leadership philosophy and not an opportunistic grab at power or authority. It set the right tone and was the foundation upon which they helped me build an even more successful, more engaged, more committed organization.

While I am not particularly comfortable with self-promotion, I received this note from a former employee, Mr. Don R. Smith, after my retirement as vice president of this division. It was given as a testimony for my leadership development seminars of my new venture, Fullsail Leadership.

I have never experienced nor worked under anyone like Bill Mayo. His unique leadership style and philosophy instilled in the employee the attitude of "I will take a long walk on a short dock for this guy." Bill never took his eye off the bottom line as far as the need for acceptable profitability and return for the shareholder, but he had an uncanny ability to address the "human side" of the workplace. Bill was actually "changing the culture" and enhancing the diversity efforts within the company. I encourage all to "get on board" for a meaningful "sailing experience."

—Don R. Smith, Caterpillar Inc.

As I've said before, we are all human leaders. And as such, we are given to make mistakes despite our best intentions. And of course there are always those on the sidelines willing to throw in their criticism, judgment, or cynicism. There is a quote that greatly inspires me when my human condition becomes all too apparent to me or to others. These words come from Teddy Roosevelt's 1910 speech entitled "The Man in the Arena."

> *It is not the critic who counts; not the man who points out how the strong man stumbles, or where the doer of deeds could have done them better. The credit belongs to the man who is actually in the arena, whose face is marred by dust and sweat and blood; who strives valiantly; who errs, who comes short again and again, because there is no effort without error and shortcoming; but who does actually strive to do the deeds; who knows great enthusiasms, the great devotions; who spends himself in a worthy cause; who at the best knows in the end the triumph of high achievement, and who at the worst, if he fails, at least fails while daring greatly, so that his place shall never be with those cold and timid souls who neither know victory or defeat.*

Roosevelt's words speak to me. And *It's a Wonderful Life* likewise has a message for everyone. It's not solely a holiday message but one that should be put into practice the entire year through. In fact, it answers Alfie's question. What's it all about? It's about love. It's about sacrifice. It's about perseverance. It's about service.

I spoke recently to an MBA class at Bradley University in Peoria, Illinois. The requested topic for my remarks was to discuss challenges for the twenty-first-century leader. In doing a little bit of research for my comments, I learned of a collaborative project between Pepperdine University and business leaders of Southern California at the turn of the twenty-first century. They conducted a survey of some eighty participating academics and business leaders to identify the perceived skills needed by the twenty-first-century leader. Fourteen categories of important attributes emerged. The participants were asked to cull that very large list to identify the top five. They successfully trimmed it to their top ten essential leadership skills, and they are listed below in order.

1. Communication and interpersonal skills

2. An ethical (or spiritual) orientation

3. The ability to manage change

4. The ability to inspire

5. Analytic and problem-solving skills

6. Being a strategic or visionary manager

7. Persistence in overcoming difficulties

8. Managing the "knowledge worker"

9. Hard Work

10. Passion

Source: Pepperdine University
Graziadio School of Business and Management

This list is now ten years old, but I doubt that it has actually changed much over the past fifty years or so of business leadership. The implications are clear. The twenty-first-century leader must be a transformational change agent able to inspire others with a compelling future vision and willing to serve with adherence to a rigorous ethical code. Like George Bailey it comes down to touching people's hearts. And as Alfie learned, that means love.

My Soft-Side Philosophical Nugget:

Why is the soft side so hard when it comes to leadership? It becomes harder than it has to be when we ignore our human capacity to love. When we view people as instruments to do work, we tend to manage them as assets. They feel controlled but not led, and their discretionary effort may be marginalized. It's said that love can move mountains. Seems a small challenge then to inspire a team. Human beings respond to human emotion. Love is the greatest of these, and therefore, the most powerful to inspire people. As Mother Teresa admonishes us, love must be put into action, and that action is service.

I've always heard it said that if you do what you love, you'll never work a day in your life. Managing is hard work. Leadership is joy and is especially joyful when you lead authentically from the heart and commit to the noble principle of service to others. You will realize results beyond what any management control can ever achieve. We speak too often of professional management when we should rather think of ourselves as amateur leaders. Why amateur? Amateur comes from the Latin word "amator," which means to love. And that's what human leadership is all about.

Epilogue: A Final Nugget

I thoroughly enjoyed working for Caterpillar, Inc. It is deserving of its accolades as one of America's most admired companies. It is world class in quality. It is an ethical firm, committed to sustainability, safety, and premium value. During my career, I was privileged to work extensively with Caterpillar dealers and thousands of Caterpillar customers directly.

In my mind, the most significant differentiating strength of Caterpillar corporate comes from its dealer network. These dealers, some 180 worldwide, are for the most part private, family-owned businesses. The average dealer in North America has been a dealer over sixty-two years. And many dealers around the world were dealers upon Caterpillar's initial incorporation in 1925. These dealers are in their second, third, sometimes fourth generation of ownership. In a hypercompetitive world, these dedicated dealers give me confidence that Caterpillar's overall performance is in good hands. I am proud of them and proud to be associated with Caterpillar, Inc., an admired global leader, making sustainable progress possible around the world.

Of course, I have written my story and have called out examples that were both positive and negative within my Caterpillar career. My admiration for Caterpillar is not in question. Business is comprised of human beings, and human beings come in all flavors. Leaders and managers do as well. I intend no offense directed to Caterpillar or its talented cadre of employees or leaders. My philosophy sometimes grated against a prevalent penchant for metrics and control, but the beauty of Caterpillar is that it gave me both the space and the privilege to practice my own brand of leadership in my own authentic way. And while rubbing up against the world of other managers created friction now and again, I honor Caterpillar for its inclusive culture that embraces a diversity of styles, leadership philosophies, and leadership implementation.

Writing a book such as this, a self-reflective philosophical muse, is fraught with a great sense of vulnerability. There is fear of exposing my weaknesses. There is anxiety that my words are not worthy of being read by others. There is a part of me that recognizes that much of my philosophy is still aspirational. I don't have all the answers. I still have many questions. After all, I'm a philosopher at heart and am prone to continually ask "why?"

As a human leader, I have learned by making my own share of mistakes, sometimes horrible mistakes. This very personal story contains my reflection and evolving philosophies about leadership over the course of my life to this point. Yet I am fully cognizant that life and my leadership learning are continual journeys. So while putting these words down and committing them to writing marks a point in time, I still recognize that I am not finished. Philosophically, my leadership is continuing to take shape. I intend to continue striving to impact others, to touch their hearts, and to leave a legacy in a new generation of leaders committed to service, to the soft side, and to authenticity.

Thank you for joining me on this reflective journey. I hope you find your true purpose and passion as a leader, and I am convinced that greatness lies within you, greatness that will be realized when you commit to leading from the heart. When you do, you'll be conducting your own unique musical score as a wonderful symphony of authenticity, service, courage, legacy, love, and let us not forget, outstanding results.

CPSIA information can be obtained at www.ICGtesting.com
Printed in the USA
LVOW06s2134071013

355893LV00002B/139/P